Christianity
in a Nutshell

Christianity in a Nutshell

LEONARDO BOFF

Translated from the Portuguese by
PHILLIP BERRYMAN

ORBIS BOOKS

Maryknoll, New York 10545

ORBIS BOOKS
Maryknoll, New York 10545

Fathers and Brothers
MARYKNOLL™

Founded in 1970, Orbis Books endeavors to publish works that enlighten the mind, nourish the spirit, and challenge the conscience. The publishing arm of the Maryknoll Fathers and Brothers, Orbis seeks to explore the global dimensions of the Christian faith and mission, to invite dialogue with diverse cultures and religious traditions, and to serve the cause of reconciliation and peace. The books published reflect the views of their authors and do not represent the official position of the Maryknoll Society. To learn more about Maryknoll and Orbis Books, please visit our website at www.maryknollsociety.org.

English translation copyright © 2013 by Orbis Books.

Originally published as *Cristianismo: O mínimo do mínimo,* © 2011 by Animus/Anima Produçoes Ltda, published by Editora Vozes, Ltda, Petrópolis, Brazil.

English translation published by Orbis Books, Box 302, Maryknoll, NY 10545–0302.

Scripture quotations translated by Leonardo Boff; English translation of scripture from the Portuguese by Phillip Berryman.

Manufactured in the United States of America.
Manuscript editing and typesetting by Joan Weber Laflamme.

Library of Congress Cataloging-in-Publication Data

Boff, Leonardo.
   Christianity in a Nutshell / Leonardo Boff ; translated from the Portuguese by Phillip Berryman.
     pages cm
    ISBN 978-1-62698-030-3 (paperback)
    1. Christianity—Essence, genius, nature. I. Title.
BT60.B5813 2013
230—dc23

                                       2013014481

To my father, Mansueto,
on his hundredth birthday;
for him the gospel was life,
and life was service to others, to the poorest.

To all those who, with or without faith,
let themselves be fascinated
by the figure of Jesus and see in him
a "treasure hidden in the field" (Mt 13:44).

Contents

Introduction   1

1. **Christianity and Mystery**   5
   1. All is Mystery 5
   2. In the beginning is communion 7
   3. The Originating Source of all being 9
   4. The great silent explosion 10
   5. Birth of the sun that supports the earth 14
   6. The universe seen from within 17
   7. The human being, infinite project 18
   8. The advent of Mystery 21
   9. The spiritualization of Mary
      by the Holy Spirit 22
   10. The incarnation of the Son in Jesus
      of Nazareth 24
   11. The personalization of the Father
      in Joseph of Nazareth 27
   12. God in all things, all things in God 30

2. **Christianity and the Ages of the Blessed Trinity**   33
   1. The era of the Spirit/Mary 33
   2. The era of the Son/Jesus 37
   3. The era of the Father/Joseph 42

3. **Christianity and Jesus**   47
   1. A root experience: The end is near 47
   2. A dream: The reign of God 53
   3. A practice: Liberation 57

4. A message: Our Father and our bread   61
5. An ethic: Unlimited love and mercy   77
6. A destiny: The execution of the liberator   81
7. An anticipation: The resurrection scarcely
   begun   83

4. **Christianity and History**   89
   1. The distinction between reign of God
      and the church   90
   2. Christianity as movement and spiritual
      way   91
   3. Christianity encountering cultures   92
   4. Christianity and the churches   93
   5. Christianity at the mercy of sacred
      and political power   95
   6. Christianity subjected to the pathologies
      of power   97
   7. Christianity from the side of the
      people   101
   8. Christianity and its reductionisms   102
   9. The future of Christianity in the age
      of globalization   107
  10. Christianity and its civilizing
      contribution   108

Conclusion: *Et tunc erit finis (All is consummated)*   **115**

Bibliography   **121**

Christianity
in a Nutshell

Introduction

Can what Christianity seeks be stated in a few words? In the more than two thousand years of its history Christianity has become enormously complicated with doctrines, theological systems, ethical codes, rituals and celebrations, and canonical and hierarchical rulings.

The ordinary Christian and even the theological community confront a special difficulty when seeking to identify a thread to connect and reconnect coherently the main items of faith and establish a hierarchy within the truths.

After fifty years of continuous intensive involvement in theological reflection, I am venturing to attempt, as a kind of swan song, to express the "minimum of the minimum," or to identify the "maximum of the minimum" of Christianity, in a way that can be understood by people who are showing some fascination for and interest in the Christian message.

I will try to express what I have to say within the contemporary worldview as it is presented to us by the earth and life sciences. That means understanding the cosmos in evolution and expansion, and for believers, sustained by the ongoing creative power of God. Out of this universe there have gradually emerged many phenomena such as, for example, the subtle articulation of cosmic energies that govern the course of the heavenly bodies, the growing complexity of orders, and finally the breakthrough of life and consciousness, and today the unification of the human species through the process of globalization.

Jesus of Nazareth himself, incarnate Son, is not foreign to this process, for he too is fruit of a long and painful trajectory of ascent and internalization to which all the elements, the cosmic energies, and the forces generating the human have contributed.

Ultimately, I am raising a simple question: How does Christianity fit into the process of the evolution of the universe that is at least 13.7 billion years old? What does it intend to reveal? What message does it bring to human beings? For believers, how does it reveal God and how is God revealed in it?

We start from a basic intuition, always affirmed by Christianity, by the mystics, and also by the most perceptive spirits of humankind: all is Mystery and all may be bearer of Mystery. This is not the limit of reason or a terrifying abyss that supplants it but an inexhaustible source of love, compassion, and acceptance.

This Mystery communicates itself and wants to be known. But astonishingly, we find that the more the Mystery is known the more it remains Mystery in all knowledge, frustrating the human desire to know ever more in an endless process. Therefore, Mystery is present here not as limit but as what is unlimited in loving reason, ever open to new discoveries and to new reasons for knowing and loving.

This source Mystery, to state it without prior mediations, is God, concealed under a thousand names attributed to God by cultures. God is Mystery, not only to us, but also to Godself, whose first essence is to be Mystery. God communicates Godself, and in doing so is revealed not as solitude but as communion of Divine Persons: the Father, the Son, and the Holy Spirit.

God creates the universe as a mirror in which God sees the divine Self and also as a vessel able to receive God when, by eternal design, God wants to communicate the divine Mystery externally. That is when God begins to be that which God eternally never was before. God knows a becoming, and thereby initiates a history.

Our presentation places (1) Christianity in relation to the source Mystery; (2) Christianity in its relationship to the Blessed Trinity and to each of the Divine Persons; (3) Christianity in connection with the figure of Jesus as the Father's Son who was incarnated; (4) Christianity in the history that followed the execution of Jesus and his personal resurrection; and finally (5) Christianity in today's history in the planetary phase of humankind.

In our exposition we have sought to maintain the dialectic inherent in history, having it show simultaneously the dimensions of light and shadows, the sym-bolic and the dia-bolic. Christianity is also involved in this dialectic. Not everything that comes in the name of Christianity is Christian.

Together with other religious and spiritual paths, it also takes part in the common mission, which is to keep alive the sacred flame of the divine Presence in each person, in history, and in the entire cosmic process. Without claiming exclusivity, but in communion with all the rest, it can present its singular message as a proposal of meaning to persons, to communities, and to the entire world, a proposal of great generosity, of inestimable spiritual greatness, and of fathomless depth toward the Mystery of the world, which ultimately comprises love, compassion, and communion of all with everyone and with all: the true name of that which we call God.

LEONARDO BOFF
Petropolis, Brazil
Easter 2011

1.

Christianity and Mystery

1. All is Mystery

Wherever we direct our gaze, to the large and to the small, outward and inward, upward or downward, an all sides we find Mystery. Albert Einstein was right when he said: "The man who does not have eyes open to Mystery will go through life seeing nothing." Mystery is not the unknown. It is that which fascinates us and draws us to know it more and more. And at the same time it arouses in us wonder and reverence. Because it is always there, It is ever there for us to know it. And when we try to know it, we recognize that our thirst and hunger for knowledge is never sated, but we can always know it more. However, at the very moment when we seize it, it eludes us toward the unknown. We pursue it unceasingly, and even so, it ever remains Mystery in all knowledge, producing in us invincible attraction, fear, and irresistible reverence. Mystery is.

In the beginning was the Mystery. The Mystery was God. God was the Mystery.

God is Mystery to us and to Godself.

God is Mystery *to us* inasmuch as we never cease apprehending it by love or intelligence. Each encounter leaves an absence that leads to another encounter. Any knowledge opens another door to new knowledge. The Mystery of God for us humans, we repeat, is not the limit to knowledge but the limitlessness of knowledge and the love that knows no rest. We never reach a situation that gives utter fulfillment. That is because Mystery neither fits into any scheme nor can it be caught in the net of some doctrine. It is ever to be known.

It is a *pro-vocative* Mystery. It always evokes, convokes, and attracts us. Whenever we perceive it for a moment, it has already escaped us, but it leaves an experience of fascination. It is an absent presence, but it is also a present absence. It is made manifest in our absolute dissatisfaction, which tirelessly and in vain seeks satisfaction. The human being is realized in this transiting between presence and absence, tragic and happy, entire but unfinished.

God is Mystery *in Godself and to Godself.* God is Mystery *in Godself* because God's nature is Mystery. Hence, God as Mystery knows Godself, and therefore God's self-knowing never ends. God is revealed to Godself and withdraws into Godself. The knowledge of God's nature as Mystery is each time entire and full, and at the same time ever open to new fullness, ever remaining eternal and infinite Mystery to Godself. Otherwise, God would not be what God is: Mystery.

God is mystery *to Godself* means that no matter how much God knows Godself, this knowledge is never exhausted. God is open to a future that really is future; therefore, something that is not yet given but that can be given as new and surprising. It is the power-to-be of Being.

But, Mystery, by an intrinsic drive, wishes to be known. It continually reveals itself and communicates itself. It goes out of itself and knows and loves the new that is manifested from itself. What will be revealed is not the reproduction of itself but always different and new likewise to Mystery itself. Different from an enigma, which upon being known is undone, the more Mystery is known the more it appears as Mystery, inviting to greater knowledge and to greater love.

To say God-Mystery is to express a drive without remainder, a life without entropy, a breaking-in without loss, an uninterrupted becoming, an eternal coming-to-be ever in being, and an ever new and different beauty that never diminishes. Mystery is Mystery, now and forever, from all eternity and for all eternity.

In the face of Mystery words are smothered, images fail, and reference points expire. What befits us is silence, reverence, adoration, and contemplation. These are the stances appropriate to Mystery.

As much as God is Mystery, we find an analogy to it within ourselves. As humans, we discover ourselves also as Mystery. No matter how much we feel ourselves, know ourselves, and love ourselves, we never succeed in knowing who we are, nor can we construct a formula that defines us, or even an image adequate to ourselves.

We are beings of utter openness: to the other, to the world, to the universe, and to God. Everything converges toward our self-knowledge, and yet we never finish knowing who we are. We do not know what we were before, what we are now, or what we will be tomorrow. We cannot know what will be revealed of us. We do not have mastery of the facts, and we are without straight-line paths moving over secure binaries. We are an infinite project seeking the Infinite, but we encounter only finites. The infinite ever recedes and hides behind every horizon we glimpse.

We are a bridge over a boundless river. Hence, we are tragic and, at the same time, blessed because we never give up, we always keep going, and we again start the pursuit of a Sun that never sets, but that is ever setting, rising, and hiding again, and is ever calling us to seek it. We are said to be images and likenesses of God for a reason. We are a Mystery of Mystery and in Mystery. We are beings aware of our own Mystery and of the Mystery of God as Mystery. This is our dignity and our destiny, our anguish, and also our fulfillment.

2. In the beginning is communion

Mystery because it is Mystery, is only accessible as Mystery, directly by God and indirectly by us, created in the image and likeness of Mystery. Nothing exists short of or beyond it, but because it is Mystery of life and movement, it continually reveals itself, pours forth out of itself, becomes accessible while remaining inaccessible Mystery. It is an ongoing simultaneous self-revelation and self-concealment. It is an eternal coming and going, a constant going forth and withdrawing.

Insofar as it remains ever inaccessible Mystery, even in self-communication and self-revelation, it is called Father. It is unfathomable, impenetrable, unthinkable. The most appropriate stance toward it is respectful and devout silence. It is an abyss of love and goodness so fascinating that it attracts all to be plunged into its paternal embrace.

The content of what is revealed by the Father in the very act of his self-communicating is called Son. He is eternally the Son of the Father. He is the Word that springs from Mystery and calls to be comprehended and welcomed. He is light from Light who illuminates all things existing and yet to exist.

Insofar as the Mystery goes out from itself (Father) and becomes Word (Son), the condition of communion of one with the other is created: Holy Spirit. This is the Breath *(spiritus)* that comes from the Father toward the Son and from the Son toward the Father, making the Three to be a single Mystery that gives itself and turns in on itself. The Spirit is the eternal energy of union within the Trinity.

Mystery does not multiply itself. It is shown as it is, as Three in eternal coexistence, in simultaneous interexistence and in perennial persistence in communion and in self-surrender of one to the other in love. That is why it is a single God.

It is the same and single Source constituted by three torrents. It is a single selfsame eternal Flame in the red at the bottom (the Father), in the yellow in the middle (the Son), and in the blue on the tip (the Holy Spirit). They intertwine, interpenetrate, and unify (become one) while not ceasing to be diverse. They are diverse in order to be able to relate and self-communicate with one another, through the other and in the other, and never without the other. Thus they are and remain eternally together.

In the beginning is not the solitude of the One but the communion of the Three. This isn't a number that can always be multiplied; the Divine Persons are unique. The unique aren't numbers; therefore, they do not add up. But they are related to one another so radically and are intertwined so completely that they emerge as a single God-communion-love. The Three are a single Source, a single eternal Fire, a single permanent Explosion and Implosion of being and coming-to-be. There is a sole God—God eternally being realized in the Person of the Father, in the Person of the Son, and in the Person of the Spirit. They are the before of the before. What has ever existed, ever exists, and ever will exist. It cannot be thought or imagined. It is the irremovable barrier to finite intelligence, which either despairs and goes crazy or surrenders in reverence to Mystery. It can be that which intelligence does not succeed in understanding.

If God-Mystery-God is always known and unknown, revealed and hidden, essentially communion and relation, then whatever comes from it will always be known and unknown. It will be relationship of all and with all, and will never be outside of relationship, which is eternal communion, and never aloneness. Being itself is always known, and at the same time, unknown. But always enmeshed in the fabric of the relationships of all with all.

3. The Originating Source of all being

Mystery in its trinitarian reality knows itself and appropriates from its overflowing reality insofar as it is self-revealed to itself. It projects what is different from it as a mirror in which the divine Three see themselves. That is the meaning of creation.

Creation reveals God to Godself. Out of the depths of Mystery emerge the infinite possibilities that are not yet realized possibilities. Hence, they are a constant newness for the trinitarian Mystery itself. Each emergence is apprehended in its totality, but another breaks in immediately, and another, and so eternally in an endless *perpetuum mobile*. The divine dynamism opens to receive them and incorporate them into its nature, and they endlessly implode and explode, making the divine essence reveal itself as uninterruptedly dynamic and display its infinite potential riches. It is newness upon newness. Surprise upon surprise. Beauty upon beauty. Understanding upon understanding. Love upon love. Passion upon passion. The God-communion has a history. It can be that which has never been before, such as, for example, the Son of the Father, who at a particular time, emerged as incarnate Son.

At a moment of its overflowing plenitude and in its desire for self-revelation and self-giving, the triune Mystery, out of its infinite possibilities and potentialities, creates a boundless ocean in ever-fluctuating waves, ocean comprised of pure energy. This is the Foundation Energy that antecedes any other thing that may come to happen. It is energy created and placed as different before the Trinity-God so that he may be seen in it and it may reveal him. It is endowed with the characteristics of Mystery without being the Mystery. It is ineffable, ungraspable, unified, and infinitely dynamic, because all its expressions have emerged after it, but it is not yet the ever irreducible Mystery. It is its image and, likewise, its best metaphor.

This vast sea of energy is pregnant with potentialities of being. Nothing is stable. It is like waves following one another unceasingly, moving onward, not held back by any boundary.

From them come flashes of energy that condense into tiny particles and then dissolve to return again into the ocean of pure energy. It is an infinite sparkle of flaming points. All is movement. All is brightness. All is effervescence. All is implosion and explosion. All is dynamic order being constituted and being undone and then being constituted again.

This ocean is a flaming Source. It is a source Flame. It is a loving abyss from which all the possible elements that will feed the universe come forth, as well as other possible universes.

It is called *Foundation Energy, Loving Abyss, Nourisher of All, Originating Source of all Being*, that sustains the entire universe, keeps every being in existence and is always available. This energy cannot be manipulated by anyone, but it can be invoked to come and flow in us.

4.   The great silent explosion

Out of that unfathomable Foundation Energy, whose reality vanishes within Mystery without being the Mystery, surprisingly and suddenly a point of unimaginable density breaks forth. It is one among so many that have emerged and have returned to the bosom of the vast ocean, but at the zero moment Mystery wanted it to collapse, that is, to take hold, be sustained, and remain. It is trillions and trillions of times smaller than the head of a pin. It is pregnant with highly condensed energy, so that its heat is billions and billions of degrees Celsius. It is Mystery in action outside of itself. Other points may also have formed by the will of the Mystery, taken hold, and exploded, creating parallel universes or existing alongside our own in another dimension.

Within this infinite point there boils a broth of pure energy virtually containing the principles, information, sub-energies, and elementary particles that will subsequently constitute the whole universe. It is there in its magnificent flashing, pulsating by the pressure of the originating energy.

Suddenly—why cannot be said—it inflated to the size of an atom and moments later, the dimensions of an apple. And then it exploded. The singularity of the Big Bang occurred. It exploded, but it was a silent thunder because there was no space and time yet to resonate, and it left a radiation so intense that it can be sensed even today in the so-called background radiation, a tiny vibration that unceasingly comes upon us from all sides of the universe. Measuring the red light of the most distant stars leads to the conclusion that that flaming Big Bang must have occurred 13.7 billion years ago. That is the age of the universe, and since we are part of it, that is our age too.

After billionths of a second of time, the energy and the foundational contents contained there are ejected violently in all directions, creating space and time. The originating energy unfolds into the four known forces: gravitational, electromagnetic, weak nuclear, and strong nuclear. What are they? To this day no satisfactory explanation has been presented, for we need them to understand all other things. That which enables us to understand all things cannot be understood. They probably show the very action of the universe, working and beginning to put order into that initial boundless disorder prompted by the Big Bang.

This originating energy strongly condensed and first produced the *Higgs field*, which constitutes the space in which the first elementary particles arose—hadrons, top quarks, protons, neutrons, electrons, positrons, and antimatter. A powerful clash then took place between matter and antimatter. The mutual destruction was so violent that only a billionth part of matter remained. Antimatter disappeared entirely. Out of that billionth of remaining matter there originated the entire vast universe that we know and that fills us with a feeling of grandeur by its magnitude.

This universe emerged out of a very subtle calibration of the four interactions that always act in combination. Had the gravitational force been the least bit too strong, all the elements would have been drawn back and would have exploded on themselves in endless explosions, possibly forming, ultimately, a black hole. The stars would have been impossible and so would life and conscious perception. Had it been by a minuscule fraction of time too weak, the expansion would be ever more diluted so as to be completely lost. Likewise, the densification of gases and elementary particles would not have happened, the great red stars would not have emerged, and life and earth would be impossible. Stephen Hawking, one of the greatest astrophysicists in the history of science, says in *A Brief History of Time* (2005): "If the electric charge of the electron had been only slightly different, stars either would have been unable to burn hydrogen and helium, or else they would not have exploded. One way or another life could not exist." Thus it has happened with each of the four forces that have acted symphonically to create the initial conditions, so that over the course of the evolutionary process the complexities, the orders, the beings bearing life and consciousness, and each of us individually, could emerge.

Energy condenses even more and gives rise to the most elementary particles that we know, the hadrons, various kinds of top quarks, protons, electrons, neurons, and ultimately atoms, and starting with atoms combined with one another, all the beings existing in the universe. Hydrogen and helium emerged, the simplest and most abundant elements in the universe.

In this regard the energy ejected together with the elementary particles formed an immeasurable cloud that expanded more and more. Slowly, after a huge explosion in all directions, it began to cool and gain density. This process led to the formation of the giant red stars.

They functioned for some billions of years, like burning furnaces within which there were atomic explosions of immeasurable magnitude. The many physical-chemical elements present in all beings were forged there: iron, sulfur, carbon, silicon, methane, gold, silver, and so forth, the more than one hundred basic elements that make up all beings and each of us. After the hydrogen and helium were consumed, they exploded. Supernovas appeared, producing a light so intense that it equals ten billion suns. They spewed out the elements inside them in all directions.

From their deaths emerged a new reality. Out of the fragments ejected were formed the galaxies, galaxy groups, stars, planets, the earth, moons, other heavenly bodies, and we ourselves, human beings. We are children of the stars and of stellar cosmic dust.

The whole evolutionary process bears within itself the initial chaos from which came the great explosion whose radiation vibrates throughout the universe. The expansion, self-organization, complexity, and ever-more-regulated orders are forms by which the universe itself tames the chaos and makes it creative. Chaos and cosmos, order and disorder, creation and destruction, sym-bolic and dia-bolic, will always coexist confront each other, and balance off, without ever reaching a final synthesis. This reality also affects the human being as simultaneously *demens* and *sapiens,* bearer of destructive energies and constructive forces. Without denying this polarization, the human being feels the ethical call to strengthen the dimension of order over that of disorder, the energy of love over the power of the negative. This situation is not a defect but a mark of each person, of each being, and of the universe itself. All obey this dynamic: chaos, order, disorder, new order, chaos, order, disorder, new order, and so forth, indefinitely. When will it culminate? We believe that the final synthesis will take place when all will be included in the kingdom of the Trinity. We await and hope.

We have just sketched the picture of creation that will allow for the Mystery to reveal itself and mirror its internal riches. At the same time this created universe will reflect the Mystery and will make itself known to us in that which can be known.

5.   Birth of the sun that supports the earth

Out of billions of galaxies, one stands out, ours, the Milky Way, spiral in form, a hundred thousand light years across.

Within it was formed a star called *Tiamat*, the *First Sun*. It shone for millions of years. Within it the elements were reworked by atomic explosions. They had previously been forged in the heart of the great red stars, which were important for the life that would emerge millions of years later with oxygen and sulfur, phosphorus, ammonia, nitrogen, and especially carbon, which is essential for the chemical combinations that allowed for life, genetic information, memory, and reflex consciousness.

After shining for millions of years, the First Sun also exploded. It became a supernova. It sent forth an immeasurable cloud of gas and elements in all directions. Slowly, however, these gasses gained consistency by the force of gravity. The sun, our sun, was born. It is now five billion years old. It was able to draw around itself the planets that formed out of the detritus from the explosion of the First Sun. One of them is earth, our Mother Earth which needed billions of years to take shape and begin to uniformly circle around the sun. It has actually existed for 4.44 billion years. Mystery gradually prepares the conditions so that going forward in millions of years of cosmogenesis, life and consciousness can break through.

For eight hundred million years it remained as a sea of fire due to its stellar origins and the meteors that brutally fell upon it, but gradually a crust took shape, making it easier for it to cool. Its suitable distance from the sun and the balance created by gravity that retained liquids created the conditions for the emergence of an atmosphere capable of welcoming life.

Life always emerges anywhere in the universe when the process of cosmogenesis (the creative genesis of the universe in expansion) reaches a certain degree of complexity and fluctuation of its elements, called chaos. Here on earth there was a proper and subtle measure of all the factors that allowed the explosion of life. Had there been a small departure from convergence, as we have said before, life as we know it would not have emerged.

Around 3.8 billion years ago the first form of life, a bacteria, emerged from a primeval ocean or from an ancestral swamp. When twenty amino acids and four nucleic acids mysteriously came together, obeying the guiding forces of the universe and the design of Mystery, life, very frail, exploded. For it to survive, the preexisting atmosphere, which was enormously hostile, was not sufficient. It had to slowly adapt and create its own habitat with its own energies and in interaction with those of earth and of the universe. This was the origin of the *biosphere*, that very thin layer that surrounds the earth and that allows all living beings to remain in existence. From this original cell have derived all forms of life, through cloning, relationships, fusions, combinations, and natural selection.

For two billion years, bacteria, viruses, and the other microorganisms multiplied by cloning and filled the whole earth. They were the *prokaryotes*, one-celled organisms with no nucleus and only a rudimentary internal organization. Because they were copied perfectly, they enjoyed and still enjoy a biological permanence.

But then a billion years after life had emerged, there appeared a cell with membrane and nucleus, a *eukaryote*. Inside it was genetic material with DNA, the formula for multiplying life. The importance of this cell comes from the fact that it was the origin of sexuality. Two cells became related and exchanged nuclei, or one merged into the other. Genetic material was then enriched with the other. Biodiversity began to emerge. Since merging could entail imperfections and small errors, diversity, and the multiplication of species, mutations, and adaptations, was fostered. Everything first happened in ocean waters and later on dry land.

Something new emerged in the Mesozoic age when the dinosaurs broke through. They were social animals who moved and hunted in groups and developed a behavior unknown in the reptile world until then. While they clashed, they cared for their eggs and the offspring after they were born until they gained independence. Later when a giant meteor crashed into the Caribbean sixty-five million years ago, they disappeared completely. They had wandered the earth for over a hundred million years.

But one of the greatest evolutionary new developments took place around 125 million years ago, when the first marsupial mammal appeared. Intimate contact with the body in gestation and living together with the offspring after birth are concomitant with the limbic brain, and with it the feelings of caring and love. This phenomenon represents a leap in the evolution of our galaxy and of the solar system. Human beings form part of the kingdom of mammals, which makes us beings of caring, feeling, and love. Life now multiplies through merging of the sexes.

Sexuality reveals relating and communion between those who are different. That fact is charged with meaning because life is structured around symbiosis, exchanges, and communion of feelings, matters, and energies. This reality intensely mirrors the source Mystery, hidden and ever revealing itself and entering into community with what is different.

With the slow emergence of the biosphere there begins a dynamic dialogue of living beings with the earth, with its energies, with its elements, and with the interactions of the universe. The biosphere is the result of this dialogue process. The primary creator has been life itself, which has ever sought and created better conditions for its own persistence and reproduction. The earth ceases to be simply a planet in the solar system. It becomes Gaia, Pacha Mama, Great Mother, a complex entity encompassing the biosphere, the atmosphere, the oceans, the mountains, soils, and ecosystems as a whole, forming a macrosystem of feedback, self-regulation, and self-regeneration, continually seeking ecological conditions favorable to life.

The already mentioned fall of a giant meteor in the Caribbean sixty-five million years ago meant a kind of great *environmental*

Armageddon. It caused the disappearance of a great portion of earthly biotic capital, but in compensation, as a kind of vendetta of the earth itself, there occurred a springtime of new forms of life that had never existed before. Until that time everything was green because of the chlorophyll produced by the ancestral forests under the kind light of the sun, which allowed for photosynthesis. Suddenly everything was filled with color. Multicolored flowers blossomed. It was the cradle that the universe prepared to be the receptacle of that ancestral being that was being announced in order to be the bearer of consciousness and of the capacity to receive the Mystery within itself: the human being, man and woman. It emerged along with the flowers; these and the shoots were its first foods.

6. The universe seen from within

We observe in cosmogenesis the following sequence: moving from energy to matter, from matter reaching life, from life attaining self-awareness, and from there the perception of the Whole and of the Mystery that sustains and permeates the whole universe. As is clear, the universe is more a magnificent thinking being than a fine machine. Consciousness, therefore, is not to be considered an alien intrusion into the world of matter. Rather, it is, as it were, the creator and regulator of matter.

This universe is not made up of the sum of all its beings. They do not exist separated from one another. All are inter-retro-connected among themselves, because everything has to do with everything, at all times and under all circumstances. The universe, therefore, is not a machine that always repeats the same movements; it is a set of all relationships interconnected and in great dynamism; it constitutes a fathomless system open to new emergences coming forth from the Foundation Energy.

The universe is accordingly always being self-organized and self-created, letting new dimensions appear. More than simply cosmos, it takes the form of a cosmogenesis. It is still in genesis; it continues being born. It is growing toward the Source from which it came, which continually attracts it so that it may be drawn into that Source. It isn't linear; it undergoes breaks, makes leaps, has phases. In other words, the university has history, and like any history the events are irreversible; they do not go back, they point forward and upward.

Presiding over the universe is a cosmogenic principle that is embodied in this logic: the more it expands, the more it enfolds on itself (complexifies); the more it folds back on itself, the more alive it appears; the more alive it appears, the more conscious it is shown to be; the more conscious it is shown to be, the more self-conscious it becomes; the more self-conscious it becomes, the more it is discovered as part of a Whole; the more it is discovered as part of a Whole, the more it discovers the Axis that unites and reunites all things; the clearer the reunifying Axis becomes in conscious-ness, the more the feelings of reverence and respect grow; the more reverence and respect grow, the more life gains meaning; and the more life gains meaning, the more is it celebrated with festivals, songs, and rituals.

All things are united in an embrace of shared life and commu-nion. The universe is self-conscious and charged with purpose. It was prepared slowly, step by step, going through terrible devasta-tions such as that of the Permian-Triassic, which took place 245 million years ago, in which a large portion of life was decimated, but with spectacular comebacks. Within this process of chaos and cosmos the forces of cosmogenesis were preparing that be-ing which was endowed with such openness that it could identify God, mixed in with all things, and accept God when God wished to communicate himself totally: man and woman, infinite project and *capax Infiniti* (capable of receiving the Infinite).

7.   The human being, infinite project

The universe prepared all the factors and found a subtle equilib-rium of all energies allowing for the emergence of the human be-ing, bearer of self-consciousness and of the perception of Mystery. But in order to be what the human being is today, *homo sapiens*

sapiens, a long route had to be taken. As there is a cosmogenesis, there is also an anthropogenesis, the genesis of the human being, man and woman, throughout the evolutionary process of the universe, of our galaxy, the Milky Way, and of earth. The human being is the end of a journey that began over thirteen billion years ago.

Simians, distant ancestors of humans, emerged seventy-five million years ago, at the end of the Mesozoic. They were small mammals, no bigger than a rat. They lived high up in gigantic trees, feeding off flowers and shoots, and ever threatened by voracious dinosaurs.

After the disappearance of the dinosaurs sixty-five million years ago, these simians could evolve unimpeded. Thirty-five million years ago we find them as primates, which formed a common trunk from which chimpanzees and other large simians emerged, on one side, and on the other side, we, beings en route to humanization. They lived in the African forests, adapting to climate changes, whether torrential rains or fierce droughts.

A decisive split occurred seven million years ago. On the one side were the large primates, chimpanzees and gorillas (99 percent of whose genes we share) in the moist and food-rich forests in Africa; on the other side, in the savannahs and dry regions, were the Australopithecines, now en route to hominization.

Three or four million years ago, in the Afar region of Ethiopia, Australopithecus displayed human-like features. Then, 2.6 million years ago there emerged *homo habilis*, who was handling tools (polished rocks and sticks) as a way of intervening in nature. A million and a half years ago it was walking on two legs; this is *homo erectus,* capable of mental operations. Alongside the 250–million-year-old reptile brain, which governs our instinctive movements, and the limbic brain formed 125 million years ago with mammals, which handles our inner universe of feelings, care, desires, and dreams, there now appeared the neocortical brain, which deals with our rationality and mental connections. And then, 200 million years ago, *homo sapiens* bursts forth, now fully human, living socially, using language and organizing subsistence cooperatively. Finally, a hundred thousand years ago, modern *homo sapiens sapiens* comes on the scene with a brain displaying such complexity that it makes this creature the bearer of conscious self-perception and a highly perceptive intelligence.

Herein is achieved the biological basis of the conscious perception that we are part of a larger Whole and that we grasp that Foundation Energy that fills the universe. We become aware of an Axis that unites and reunites all things and with which we can commune through rituals, dances, singing, and speaking.

Having emerged in Africa, these humans will begin their pilgrimage through the continents until they occupy the whole planet down to our own time. Starting in the Neolithic, around ten thousand years ago, they begin to live socially in an organized manner. They build villages, cities, states, cultures, and civilizations. They ponder the meaning of their life, their death, and the universe, as is evident in the stone graffiti and paintings in various parts of the world. They organize worldviews around that powerful and loving Energy that sustains and permeates everything. They discover themselves as beings open to wholeness and inhabited by an infinite desire. Mystery becomes more and more sacramental; that is, it is announced ever more perceptibly in human consciousness.

Human beings translate their experience of Mystery with myriad names born out of their reverence, ecstasy, and love. They feel immersed in this Mystery that gives them meaning in life. They open to the world around them, to the other, to different societies, to the All, and to God. Nothing satiates them. Their cry for plenitude echoes the voice of the Mystery that calls them to communion. Humans can be companions in love, hearers of the Word, hosts of Mystery within themselves. The human being can incarnate the Triune God, and the Triune God can become incarnate in the human being. The conditions for this were given over the course of anthropogenesis. Human beings are an infinite openness that calls out for the infinite. They seek it insatiably everywhere and under all forms, and find only finites. What infinite will come to meet them and fill them? An infinite emptiness demands an Infinite Object that will give it plenitude. Then they will have the experience of Augustine and finally rest in God.

8. The advent of Mystery

Two impulses meet: that of Mystery, which wishes to communicate itself and be completely in the other, and that of human beings, who are completely open to Mystery in which they want to rest fully and find the supreme realization of their search for the Infinite.

In communicating itself, Mystery, which is the Trinity of the Divine Persons, goes out of itself completely toward the human being. Mystery empties itself in order to be completely in the other. Mystery becomes the other.

In welcoming the self-communication of Mystery, human begins completely empty themselves of themselves in order to be all in Mystery. They become Mystery in the manner possible to them as creatures.

When the encounter of these two outgoings takes place, one toward the other, in such a way that Mystery becomes the other and the other becomes Mystery, then Mystery is fully hominized and the human being is completely divinized.

Mystery, present in the Foundation Energy, was always communicating itself in the evolutionary process, being present in each being and in its unique way of being realized in the energies, in the elementary particles taken as vibrating strings, in the celestial bodies, in galaxy groups, in the stars, in the planets, in minerals, in bacteria, in complex cells, in every living being, in reptiles, in mammals, in self-conscious beings. It penetrated into all of them, and they penetrated into it. It was the inclusive embrace of Mystery with its creation.

But a new level was reached when Mystery was entrusted completely to the self-conscious and free human being. At each stage it began to be that which it was not. It continually revealed itself to itself as it gave itself to others.

But the greatest self-giving and also the greatest acceptance occurred in the human being. Mystery itself created a subject in which there dwelt an infinite yearning, capable of welcoming the

Infinite, open to hosting Mystery. The entire universe moved in this direction, stage by stage, order by order, complexity by complexity, until finally there burst forth that creature which, not being Mystery, could be identified with Mystery.

That was when the complete personalization, incarnation, and spiritualization of Mystery as Trinity took place: Father, Son, and Holy Spirit.

Since the Triune God is one and the Divine Persons are always found interwoven, so that they always act in communion, when they self-communicate they do so as they really are: as Trinity. The entire Trinity goes out of itself, externalizes itself, and permeates that which it has created, fit for receiving it.

Since this being does not exist in itself and for itself but always in relation to all other beings, and since it is the fruit of the entire process of evolution, it then means that the totality of the universe and each of the beings was touched by the advent of Mystery, of the Blessed Trinity. The universe became the great mirror in which the Trinity sees itself. It was transformed into the most holy temple, which welcomed and hosted the Trinity. When this happens, the happy end of all creation is anticipated. It has become the body of the Trinity.

9.   The spiritualization of Mary by the Holy Spirit

The three Divine Persons, by reason of the radical inter-retro-relationship that they have among themselves, always act together. Everything in them is common, except for the fact that they are distinct, that is, one is not the other, but they are distinct in order to be able to surrender themselves reciprocally, to live communion, and to be together. Thus they unify; that is, they are a single God-Trinity.

What is third in the reign of the Trinity is first in the reign of creation. Thus, in its incarnational will Mystery in the Person of the Holy Spirit was the first to go out of itself and to pitch its tent among humans. The divine Three are present there, but through a similarity with creation, it is the Holy Spirit who best expresses Mystery, entering into creation. It is the moment of welcoming and receiving what is different within Mystery, for the great nuptial of creation with its Creator. It is the moment of the great integration.

The Spirit presents dimensions of the feminine: it generates life, cares for every being, arouses the new, and lovingly welcomes creation in itself. In Semitic languages the Spirit is the female, generating principle.

Miriam of Nazareth, a simple woman of the people, humble, completely open to Mystery because she is "full of grace" (Lk 1:28), valiant like a prophetess in appealing for God's intervention to "cast down the powerful from their throne and fill the hungry with good things" (Lk 1:52–53), was prepared to welcome the Holy Spirit inside herself.

That is why, at a particular moment of history, the "Holy Spirit came over her and pitched its tent in her" (Lk 1:35). That is, the Spirit came, did not go away, and has remained in her permanently. The Spirit wished to dwell with her definitively and become one with her.

And Mary said: *Fiat,* "Be it done" (Lk 1:38). From that moment, the Spirit who hovered over the primordial chaos out of which came all beings, that Spirit who was pushing all things upward and forward, that Spirit who permeated all matter and complexified it, that Spirit who caused life to explode, that Spirit who in mammals aroused feeling, care, and love, that Spirit who lit up the human spirit so that it could understand the logic of evolution, that Spirit who made prophets cry out, poets sing, inventors create, that Spirit who sowed love, friendship, benevolence, the feeling of justice, compassion, mercy, and the supreme gift of self-giving to the other in love, that Spirit, as of now, is fully in a woman and through her enlivens everything with energy, vigor, kindness, and love.

As the Spirit came to her, she went to meet the Spirit. She kept opening herself to everything that was devotion, kindness, and loving. She felt that God "was with her" (Lk 1:28). The encounter between the woman and the Spirit took place; the motherly, wifely, friendly face of God was revealed. The welcoming and generating feminine, throughout the millions and millions of years of evolution, reached a high point. Now Mary was spiritualized, identified with the Spirit. The Spirit was feminized and was united to Mary forever, and with her to the feminine in creation and female humankind.

This Spirit is fruitful and has generated in her a child who will be the incarnation of the Son. At a moment in history the center is occupied by a woman. The Spirit is in her, and the holy humanity of the eternal Son grows within her. Over her operates mysteriously the Father whose Son was conceived in the power of the Spirit. She is the temple of the most holy Mystery. The Spirit became woman. The woman became Spirit.

10. The incarnation of the Son in Jesus of Nazareth

The Holy Spirit dwells in the young woman Miriam of Nazareth. Although she is a virgin, she feels within herself—strangely—a generating Energy. It is the action of the Spirit. A new life begins to form within her. Perplexed, she says, "How is it possible, if I do not know man?" (Lk 1:34). But she overcomes her natural reluctance, for she becomes aware of the Spirit with whom she enjoys a deep intimacy. He is showing his creative power as at the first moment of creation. She surely understands nothing, but she feels privileged and "blessed among all women" (Lk 1:42). "Who is this new child hidden in my womb? What Mystery am I carrying within myself?" She pondered these questions and kept them in her heart (Lk 2:51).

In the power of the Spirit, Mary conceived a little boy inside herself. The energies of the entire universe converged on him. Each element was virtually present in that tiniest primordial point that then exploded, all the materials that were forged in the heart of the giant red stars, the galaxies, the stars, the earth, the other heavenly bodies, the more complex orders that gave rise to life, the more ordered forms of life that reached the self-perception of themselves; indeed, everything has constituted a huge cradle to welcome this child who is slowly growing until he is born.

His name is Jesus of Nazareth. From his first moment he is seen to be *capax Infiniti*. In fact, he welcomed it fully, insofar as his life was manifested as child, as youth, and as adult. At each phase the Son is present in accordance with the capacity of the phase in question. In him the eternal Son set up his permanent dwelling (Jn 1:14). He is incarnated in this man of Nazareth, a village so insignificant that it is not even named in the First Testament. He grows up like any child, youth, and adult man. He goes through the crises entailed in each phase, confronting them, and that is how he matures and shapes his identity as man. His name, Jesus, is not found in any chronicle from the time. He is an unknown. He learns the profession of his father, an artisan, a jack-of-all-trades who puts up roofs, raises walls, builds household items like tables, chairs, and wheels, and at the same time works as a farmer to assure food for the family, as was the custom of all artisans.

But in him dwells the eternal Son, he who is the Word by which Mystery leaves behind its hidden character and makes itself known. The Son is not incarnated as a king, or as a high priest, or as a sage knowledgeable about the scriptures and the things of the world. He becomes our flesh, that is, our miserable and vulnerable human condition, and "subject to weakness" (Heb 5:2), but also hardworking, determined, and full of projects. He is familiar with joys and sorrows, indignation and piety, and "learned obedience through what he suffered" (Heb 5:8). He is like us in all things, but there is a difference: he is entirely and completely open to receiving the Son when the latter wants to communicate himself. At each moment and at each stage of his personal evolution, he opens himself to the coming of the Son. The Son is in him and accompanies him. He went on growing from within the process of evolution until he burst forth within it.

Because he is the incarnate Son, he feels God as *Abba*-Papa. The only one who can cry out "*Abba*-Papa" is he who feels he is really Son, and Son in an absolute sense, that is, without any other qualification. Surely, it is the first time in our galaxy, in our solar system, and on our earth, that someone has an awareness of being Son of God-*Papa*. The two movements meet: the Son, who within evolving matter is externalizing himself and ascending, is incarnated and becomes man, and Jesus, who welcomes, internalizes, and opens up completely to the Son, becomes Son of the Father. In his life, word, and work he reveals the hidden Mystery, now revealed in human form. As Son he feels that the "Father works and that he works with him" (Jn 5:17). In feeling that he is Son of *Abba*-God, he created the possibility of each human being, man and woman, also feeling that he or she is son or daughter of God, for we all bear the same human nature that he bore. If human nature is touched by the Son, all members of this nature share in the Son and also become sons and daughters of God in the Son. It is the high point of the awareness and the perception of the dignity of the human being.

His intention is to proclaim a dream: that of the reign of God. It is the absolute revolution that transforms all things and aligns them to the design of Mystery. The one who is sick is cured; the one who is lost is found; the one who has sinned against God experiences divine mercy. Even the wind and sea obey him (Mk 4:39). He shows power over the shadowy aspects of existence: sickness, despair, and death. In him things begin to be renewed. The reign was brought near (Mk 1:15) and began a process that will end only in the transfiguration of all things.

But a tragedy pursues him: "He came for what was his, and his own did not receive him" (Jn 1:11). What he presented was too new and required radical changes. He entered into dangerous confrontations with the religious and imperial authorities, who led him to the most shameful punishment imposed on a person: crucifixion. He was executed. He did not die a natural death like a wise old rabbi, surrounded by disciples. Death was imposed on him as condemnation. Acceptance of judicial murder was not easy for him, because it meant that his dream was not being realized. That is why he is understood to have cried out on the cross in desperation: "Eloi, Eloi, lema sabachthani!" (My God, my God, why have you abandoned me?) Even so, he is despoiled completely of himself, his faith, his hope, and his dream. He surrenders to the nameless Mystery: "Father, into your hands I commend my Spirit" (Lk 23:46). The evangelist Mark expresses how dramatic the moment is: "Giving a great sigh, he expired" (14:34).

But God did not abandon him. Jesus realized the dream of the reign in his person. After having emptied himself completely, he can also be completely fulfilled. The Father and the Spirit resurrected him, but it is a resurrection that was limited just to his person, indirectly touching humankind and creation to which he is bound, and which remains in the old order. Resurrection provides a convincing inaugural sign that the dream was not empty and that it continues in the form of hope and of historic process. The one who resurrects is a failure, broken by torture and disfigured by the crucifixion. That fact signals a promise that the reign also begins to be realized in all those who have had the same fate as Jesus: those unjustly humiliated and offended. They are his brothers and sisters in suffering, and they will be the first to share in his new life.

The resurrection is personal, but because the Risen One is part of the universe and of the earth, it indirectly acquires an earthly and cosmic dimension: all the elements of the universe are touched by this incipient transfiguration. A revolution in evolution has begun, but it is barely the beginning. The future is still open. The incarnate Son, limited to the space of Palestine, through the resurrection has become the cosmic Christ, filling all spaces in the universe. Saint Paul, enthusiastically and with certain excitement, will say that he is *panta en pasin,* that is, "all in all things" (Col 3:11). The universe bears within itself a most powerful Energy of animation, cohesion, and synthesization, which is the Risen Christ. The reign that was near and that is in our midst, displays, seminally and initially, its transforming action in the person of Jesus.

11. The personalization of the Father in Joseph of Nazareth

The entire Trinity-God communicated itself and came to its creation, breaking in from within. Creation was conceived to be the body of the Trinity. The Spirit came, and the Son was incarnated. Now it is the Father who breaks in within his creation, which he sustains and makes evolve at each moment.

Although the Divine Persons always act together, there are actions that are more akin to, and have therefore been appropriated to, one of the Persons, in this instance to the Father. Thus, all are the Mystery that wishes to reveal and communicate itself, but in the Person of the Father, Mystery appears more as Mystery insofar as Mystery, that is, as always hidden and irreducible. The Father is ineffable but is always Father of the Son in the power of the Holy Spirit. The Father does not speak; it is the Son, the Word, who speaks. The Father works (Jn 5:17), and to him is attributed creation; ordering it and enlivening it falls to the Spirit. It is through creative action that the Father goes forth from his Mystery and is gradually revealed in creation as it evolves, while ever remaining Mystery.

In one person in human history, in Joseph, the Father projected someone who could express his character of Mystery and of worker in his creation. This person does not speak or say words; he speaks through hands that work. He only dreams. Dream is the dimension of depth and of the inaccessible. That is where Mystery has its home. He uses his hands as a Mediterranean artisan, woodworker, and farmer. He is deeply pious to the point where he is a model for the whole community; that is why everyone regards him as "just," an expression that at that time meant being very much a part of the community, with clear signs of wisdom and virtues.

He was a widower with several children, whom the gospels call brothers of Jesus (Jn 7:3, 5). Their names are known: James and Joseph, Simon and Jude (Mt 13:54). He met a young girl showing signs of pregnancy. Fearing the rumor mongers in the village, where everyone knows everything about everyone, and the discrimination that she might endure for looking pregnant, out of compassion, he took her to his house. He married her. He took on the son who would be born. The symbol of this in Jewish culture is to impose on him the name Jesus. He thereby becomes father of the child with the responsibilities incumbent on a father: to provide for the necessities of the house, take care of his education, introduce him into the traditions of the people, have him take part in religious and secular celebrations such as a wedding, and teach him his own profession as craftsman and farmer.

His name is Joseph, Joseph of Nazareth. He lives his mission as father so deeply that he experiences God as the great and mysterious Father. With the Father he enjoys such intimacy that he then passes it on to his son Jesus, who later begins to call God

"*Abba*-Papa." Jesus can only call God *Abba* because Joseph lived this intimate dimension of a kind and tender father. Without the experience of Joseph as *Abba*, it is unlikely that Jesus would have called his God *Abba*-Father. That was his root experience.

The entire universe was prepared for this person to have such a radical feeling. He felt united to the Father, but so united that he experienced an identification with him: Father with father. Indeed, Joseph represents all fathers in history, who by the fact of being fathers have experienced God as good and loving Father, alongside other forms of experience. Every father, in the past, the present, and the future, in Palestine, India, China, Brazil, the Andes, the North and South Pole, experiences God as Father in some fashion. In each of these fathers the heavenly Father becomes present in his own and different form, and is preparing his full and complete coming in Joseph.

That blessed event took place in the person of Joseph. The Father was identified with Joseph. Two movements again came together there: the Father broke into the person of Joseph in his fatherhood, which he assumed as his own; and Joseph plunged into the fatherhood of the Father so completely that he felt identified with him. The Father was personalized in Joseph, and Joseph was paternalized in the Father.

Here we have the supreme glory: in some obscure corner of Palestine, far from the centers where history is taking place, news circulates, and the chroniclers make observations, there was a person who reached the highest degree of his experience of Mystery as Source and Origin of all. He lived out his mission as a providing, caring, educating, and working father and husband so radically that in him there broke forth the awareness that God is also Father, a Father kind and loving, whom he intimately experienced as *Abba*-Papa.

Now the Father is among us through Joseph. That powerful Energy that creates and sustains all, that permeates the entire universe and each being from point to point, is now personalized in the historic figure of the anonymous widower, craftsman, and peasant, Joseph. His figure is so mysterious that we do not even know who his father was—Matthew says it was Jacob (1:16) and Luke, Heli

(3:23)—or where he was born or when he died. He is a mystery, apt for personally representing the Mystery who is the Father.

Whether he was or was not aware of this blessed fact is not important; what is important is that the Father worked this marvel in him, personalizing himself in him, making him experience God as Father, to the point of feeling radically united to him. It suffices for us to profess: Joseph is the earthly personification of the heavenly Father, and the Father is personalized in the earthly father Joseph.

12. God in all things, all things in God

At the end of our rise toward communion as Mystery and of the incursion of Mystery into the evolving universe, we discover that we are all in Mystery and that Mystery is in us. We are Mystery by participation.

We call this presence, in which each retains its own identity, *panentheism*. Panentheism—which should not be confused with pantheism—means that God-Mystery is in the innermost recess of each being, and that each being is innermost in God-Mystery. All is perichoretic; that is, everything is involved in *perichoresis* (inter-retro-penetration), which is the existence of all with all, with God, by God, for God, and through God. And God-Mystery realizes its Mystery with the universe, through the universe, and for the universe; the universe ever remains universe and God-Mystery ever God-Mystery. But they will be forever intertwined and will be eternally in communion. There is no separation, only distinction. There is no chasm placed between because there are bridges and networks of inclusive relationships everywhere. The *pantheist* understanding works differently—all is God, with no differentiation. The rock is God, the sea is God, the animal is God, the human being is God. Here differences are extinguished, and that may lead to absurdities. In *panentheism* the differences between Creator and creature are affirmed, but the presence of one in the other is so great that despite the differences they are always in communion with and in one another.

There is a line that is internal and that opens from within outward: Mary, wife of Joseph and mother of Jesus, externalized the
Holy Spirit and now, by his power, has been introduced into the
reign of the Trinity and is seen to be radiant, identified with him.
The feminine is divinized and eternalized. Jesus, son of Mary and
of Joseph, has externalized the Son through the incarnation, and
having risen lives transfigured in the reign of the Trinity. The male
has gained its ultimate and eternal setting. Joseph, Jesus' father
and Mary's husband, externalized the Father in being personally
assumed by the eternal Father and lives his fatherhood to the utmost in the reign of the Trinity. In short, through them and with
them the first fruits of the universe have reached the root Source
of all being.

There is another line, which is external, from outside inward:
The Spirit came to dwell definitively in a woman, was spiritualized,
was internalized in her, and eternalized all the female in creation.
Through incarnation the Son was internalized in Jesus of Nazareth
and through him all human beings, all the elements of the universe,
began to be divinized, and the male began to become part of God.
The Father was internalized through his personalization in Joseph
of Nazareth, making all universal fatherhood express the source
Mystery of the Father. The heavenly Trinity was internalized in
the earthly Trinity. The divine family entered history in the human
family. Trinity-God, as it is, is fully and without remainder, among
us; it came from its eternal world and was received by Mary, Jesus,
and Joseph in their temporal world.

This event of infinite tenderness is lived under the shadow
proper to Mystery. It shares in the ups and downs of the evolutionary process, painfully recovers from the mass decimations,
and has jubilantly triumphed over the destructive force of chaos,
transforming itself into life-giving power. Cosmos was finally born
from chaos.

Et tunc erit finis. "And then will come the end" when all will
culminate. The God-Mystery who was externalized, who became
other, who became non-Mystery, and who went into exile, re-
turns over itself, bearing with it the history of the universe, which

expanded, created itself, organized itself, and transcended itself. Now there exists only the reign of the Trinity, within which is the created other that has enabled Mystery to show itself as Mystery, to become that which it never has been before, and to enrich its every hidden essence as mystery, ever open to receive, take on, and make God-Trinity be all in all things.

2.

Christianity and the Ages of the Blessed Trinity

The Spirit sleeps in the rock
Dreams in the flower
Feels in the animal
Knows that he feels in the man
Feels that he knows in the woman.

1. The era of the Spirit/Mary

What is third in the internal order of the Trinity, the Holy Spirit, becomes first in the external order of creation. The whole Trinity comes down and enters into history. But the first to touch the fringes of the created was the Holy Spirit. And rightly so, for he is the *Spiritus Creator et Ordinator*, the one who hovered over the *tohuwabohu*, over the originating chaos, and from there set in motion all the elementary energies and particles that allowed for all beings and all orders within evolution. He is the Originating Source who nourishes,, sustains, permeates, pushes, and pulls the entire cosmogenic process toward a culmination still to be achieved and revealed.

Everything having to do with love as the force of fascination, attraction, and union, with the solidarity that includes all, with the forgiveness that reconciles, with the communion that binds and reconnects all, with creative fantasy, innovation, invention, creation, extrapolation, transcendence, ecstasy, newness, complexity, order, beauty, and with the most varied forms of life, has to do with the Spirit. Inspiration is the work of the Spirit. The enthusiasm by which initiatives are taken is action of the Spirit. Resistance and resilience is the power of the Spirit in action. The ecstasy that makes the human extrapolate and reach the highest levels of consciousness is the breaking-in of the Spirit. Plunging into the depths of the Self is led by the Spirit. The top quark string, which trembles in trillions of vibrations per second, energies that are interconnected, the new beings that emerge in the evolution are all effervescence of the Spirit. He creates diversity and is responsible for unity. The multiplicity of beings and of gifts in humans through the power of the Spirit converge toward union, cooperation, and communion.

The action of the Spirit reached its high point in Mary's womb, after her *fiat*, when he began to produce the holy humanity of Jesus of Nazareth. The Spirit accompanied him his entire life, opened his mind to the world, was active as he overcame the crises proper to youth and the choice of his direction in life, and opened to him the meaning of the dream that he set out to proclaim: the reign of God. In the power of the Spirit, Jesus did marvelous works: from changing water into wine (Jn 2:9), to raising his friend Lazarus from the dead (Jn 11:44). The Spirit especially prompted Jesus to feel his God as *Abba*-Papa, and on that basis he passed on that experience to all human beings.

The Spirit fills the universe and the face of the earth. It blows where it will (Jn 3:8). Missionaries always arrive later, for the Spirit was there before them, in history and in the heart of peoples. In them he was stirring up love, forgiveness, solidarity, kindness, and care for everything that lives and breathes. In them he prompted the emergence of languages, the arts, music, monuments, and cuisines. Through him sages taught and mystics penetrated into the Mystery of God.

The Spirit awakened the feminine dimensions of God in creation: love, care, solidarity, sensitivity to everything living, the ability to grasp the messages that come to us from everywhere in the universe, from nature, from the earth and from every human person, the feeling of collaboration and of suffering for others, the power of generating and caring for the least sign of life, the sense of beauty and aesthetics, of enchantment, exaltation, pure and innocent joy and its capacity for grasping the invisible and feeling God through the body. All are manifestations of the Spirit, who in Middle Eastern and many other cultures was perceived as divine energy of the female Entity.

The supreme work of the Spirit was being lovingly identified with Mary. He dwelled definitively in her. He was internalized in her. He became Mary, allowed her to become Spirit, for she identified with Him. There was a total and complete outpouring of the Spirit in creation, and through Mary there was an ultimate interpenetration of creation in the Spirit. Since Mary is part of the cosmos and all the energies, particles, and information present in the universe are present in her, the entire cosmos and the earth have been touched by the Spirit.

The cosmos is en route to its culmination. Its ascent takes place in the interplay of chaos and cosmos, disorder and order, creation and destruction, ever allowing the emergence of new orders and complexities increasingly charged with purpose. It is the work of the Spirit to assure that cosmos always triumphs, that order overcomes disorder, and complexity produces new beings. The Spirit always has to do with the future. He is the principle of the new heavens and new earth. When he enters into all of evolution "the wilderness shall become a fruitful field, and the fruitful field . . . a forest. Then justice will dwell in the wilderness, and righteousness abide in the fruitful field. The effect of righteousness will be peace, and the result of righteousness, quietness and trust forever" (Is 32:15–17). New birth is attributed to the Spirit (Jn 3:3–8). We encounter a growing spiritualization of all creation, filled with dynamism, life, and communion of all with all and with Trinity-God. Creation will now be a system fully open to accepting and enjoying mystical union with the Inexhaustible Source of all Being, ever new and ever surprising. It is more than sharing in the life of Trinity-God, it is a plunge into living from God: an infinite process of self-revelation and of self-realization in which we are included as the created portion.

One of the great works of the Spirit has been that of not allowing Jesus' dream of the reign of God to die. It was the Spirit who enlivened the apostles desolated by the failure of Jesus. He poured into them an unexpected and surprising energy for continuing to proclaim what Jesus proclaimed and did. The church as community of the faithful as we have it today is as much fruit of the Spirit as of Jesus. Jesus was seeking the reign and did not intend the church, but with his death a vacuum was created, as clearly shown in the words of the young men of Emmaus. They were hoping that he had come to save the people, but regrettably he has died miserably on the cross (Lk 24:20). It is the Spirit who comes and fills this vacuum, generating communities that propose to follow Jesus and attempt to make real his dream of the reign. They are not the reign, but they allow themselves to be inspired by the reign proclaimed by Jesus.

Without the Spirit there would be no way to understand the resonance achieved by Jesus in subsequent history. It was the Spirit who led the communities to discover that beneath that weak man of working-class stock, itinerant prophet, was indeed hidden the incarnate Son of the Father. This discovery is still being made to this day by each generation. We only regret that the manner in which the Son of the Father has been revealed in history, in anonymity and humility, is not respected. He began to be exalted so disproportionately, to the point where Jesus of Nazareth was no longer recognizable. The Christ of faith swallowed up the Jesus of history. This development has brought problems down to our own time. The Son became warm and mortal flesh. Institutional theology has turned the flesh into a transcendent spirit far removed from the concrete human condition. Hence, the Spirit himself helps us to rescue Jesus of Nazareth, the incarnation of the Son of the Father in our misery. We can say whatever we want of Christ, but we cannot deny the fact and the truth that the Son of the Father became incarnate in our contradictory human condition, marked by a thousand limitations, anxieties, and joys. He was a poor man among the poor, not a priest among the priests or a scribe among the scribes. As the poet Fernando Pessoa writes in "Freedom": "Jesus understood nothing of finances, and there's no evidence that he had a library."

2. The era of the Son/Jesus

Jesus,
I praise you a thousand times
Because you were rebellious
Struggling day and night,
Against the injustice of humanity.

—Nicaraguan Peasant Mass

The era of the Son is what has become most visible in history. It is of the nature of the Son to be the revealer of the Mystery and hence that Person who stands out most because he penetrates into the most radical obscurities of matter and takes root in history through incarnation in the man Jesus of Nazareth.

The historical Jesus would probably not recognize anything that they have done with him after his life, death, and resurrection. As a humble craftsman, farmer, itinerant prophet, suffering servant, he would feel strange in the face of all the titles added to him, coming especially from the realm that he most criticized and condemned: that of power. He would be scandalized and would vehemently condemn, maybe with whip in hand, the pomp and palatial magnificence of those who claim to be his direct representatives and who preside over the Christian community bureaucratically and without love. It would not be on such excrescences that his church would be built, but on his faithfulness to God-*Abba* to the end; on his dream of the reign of God, which is intended first of all for the poor and oppressed; on some powerful signs that he always did on behalf of life, especially for those suffering most; and primarily on his resurrection. Such events made it possible to believe and hope: all would not end on the cross. Something of the reign did not succumb when its proclaimer was eliminated; it was achieved at least seminally in his person.

A historic space was thereby opened for the emergence of followers and communities to take his cause forward. Now it is no longer the apocalyptic mindset, that of the Jesus of history, that will predominate, but that of history, open to the future, of mission, and of the conversion of people, as illustrated in exemplary fashion in the Acts of the Apostles. This concern for spreading the message and the meaning of the person of Jesus led to the emergence of *Christology*. It is an intellectual effort to ponder more deeply the significance of the deeds of Jesus, at the risk of forgetting his lowly origins and falling into the process common at that time, that of exalting figures considered historic. A great deal of Christology has succumbed to this danger, rendering the historical Jesus almost unrecognizable. Christology is done at the expense of "Jesusology."

Christology followed more or less the following course: It began by attributing to Jesus the more modest and human titles of Master, Prophet, just, good, holy. Then came more sublime and divine titles like Son of Man, Messiah-Christ, Son of God, Lord, New Adam, Savior of the World, Head of the Cosmos, and by the end of the first century, with the evangelist John, even God himself. In a short space of fifty years from his execution Christian thinkers caused almost all of these divine and human titles of glory and honor existing in Judaic, Hellenistic, and imperial culture to be attributed to Jesus. On the basis of this process of exaltation his whole story was reread, and a supernatural and divine aura was created even around his humble birth, which very probably took place in Nazareth rather than in Bethlehem. This strategy of exaltation, which contradicts the anonymous origins of the prophet and suffering savior, was taken forward systematically by those who held power in the communities. Manuscripts circulated with his sayings, others with miracle accounts, and yet others with his parables, and a longer document narrating the passion, crucifixion, and resurrection. All this vast material took on literary form in the four gospel books of Mark, Matthew, Luke, and John. Their genre is not written history; that is, they did not intend to write a biography but to give testimony and to proselytize (in the good sense of the word, seeking to make known) the life, work, and message of Jesus and to win over followers. For that purpose all the elements listed above were sewn together and combined, but within the framework of an astounding deep theological reflection. From it came the four books called Gospels, a literature very much committed to proclaiming and exalting Jesus of Nazareth, each emphasizing a different perspective corresponding to the idea prevailing in the communities where they came to maturity.

Running parallel to this process of exaltation was another one linked to the memory of Jesus' origins in poverty. It is grassroots Christianity, which has always existed through history. Its bearers have cultivated the image of Jesus as wandering prophet, storyteller, healer, displaying freedom in the face of the prevailing traditions and rituals, persecuted and calumniated preacher, threatened with death. The central figure is the cross and the Crucified One. Little is said of the resurrection, seen apologetically as proof that Jesus was God. This tradition has produced a spirituality of following Jesus in humility and in total surrender to the Father. Continually enriched with new cultural elements, it has created the history of piety around the veneration and adoration of Jesus. It has found its expression in history in male and female religious life and in different versions of monasticism, but it has become remarkably central in the poor and enslaved strata of ordinary people, especially in countries colonized by Europeans. They have seen in the suffering, tortured, and crucified Jesus their own situation as exploited or in slavery. This is people's Catholicism, which ought to be understood in its proper value, within the parameters of popular culture rather than as a debased form of so-called official Christianity.

In any case, with pluses and minuses, the figure of Jesus became a fundamental archetype of the human condition in pursuit of redemption and the brightest feature of Western culture. It has thereby penetrated into the collective unconscious and begun to be understood no longer as the possession of the churches and of the Western world but rather of all humankind. Having become an archetype, it is ever reemerging under different names, forms, and meanings.

What was the great work of the Son Jesus for humankind and for the evolutionary process? *First*, to extend to all humans the awareness that they are sons and daughters of God. This is the supreme dignity that raises up the human being above all things, structures, and types of power. As son and daughter the human being stands immediately before God, with no further mediation. *Second*, it has made it possible to draw the consequences of our being sons and daughters of God: we are in fact naturally all brothers and sisters of one another; here differences of place of origin, social status, privileges, and reasons for discrimination are worthless. All are placed on a single level of brotherhood and sisterhood. That standpoint is the basis for a new ethic: treating humans humanely because they are brothers and sisters. *Third*, the fact that we are sons and daughters, brothers and sisters, confers on us an incomparable dignity and sacredness that finds its ultimate root and justification in God. All are worthy, sacred, and untouchable because all are marked by God the Son. They bear within themselves the potentiality of also being assumed by the Son so as to begin to be part of the divine family. *Fourth*, this set of values has provided the basis for a kind of common shared life that seeks to be governed by equality, fairness, justice, and kinship. These values are present in the foundation of democracy. *Fifth*, Saint Francis of Assisi is celebrated because in the thirteenth century he radically lived the following of Jesus and the mystery of the incarnation: perceiving the cosmic dimension of universal kinship. If all come from the same Father and all are brothers and sisters of the Son of God, then other creatures also have God as Father and are our brothers and sisters, from the snail laboriously crossing the road, to the sun, the moon, and the most distant stars; that is why there is an earthly and cosmic kinship. Human beings are not shut up in their tiny human world; they live with the great community of life and include in their love all beings of creation. Everything is Christified. Indeed, the incarnation of the Son of God in our lowliness means nothing else but this: we all belong to the divine family, we are of the Trinity-God; when we come to the end of our days, the Son himself comes seeking us and will take us to the home where we always belong. And there we will live eternally divinized.

On the basis of this experience of a cosmic kinship, the medieval Franciscan masters, and in modern times others under the influence of Pierre Teilhard de Chardin, have worked out their theologies in which Christ is not seen as reduced to the space of Palestine, or confined to the human world, but rather seen within the Mystery of creation, in the very process of the universe. From the first moment in which matter emerged, Jesus was there seminally, and he kept growing and advancing through the various stages of evolution, experiencing its retreats and advances, until finally it breaks into the consciousness of a poor farmer and craftsman that he is Son of *Abba*-God. In a hidden manner he is the cosmic Christ, whose Christic energy remains present in evolving matter. Jesus of Nazareth surely knew nothing about this, nor did he need to know it. These dimensions went much beyond his possible awareness. It suffices that the Son had made Jesus the subject capable of receiving him when he resolved to emerge from matter and fully communicate himself, but he did not communicate as one who has invaded the other's space. He assumed someone who felt himself to be Son because he invoked God as *Abba*-Papa, he became a being-for-others, he put himself at the service of a dream, understood as God's great intention: the reign. This human being, Jesus who feels himself as Son, is already the presence of the incarnate Son. Then the Son became Jesus. Jesus became the Son. The internalization of the Son of God in human history took place in anonymity and in the darkness of an everyday human life, far from theological circles and the futile chatter that characterizes the court palaces of the powerful and religious curias.

The incarnation of the Son took place in Jesus, who was rejected along with his cause, the reign. What followed was Christianity. It also followed the logic of incarnation in people, in the various cultures and languages, and in philosophies and worldviews. Thus, it was incarnated in doctrinal expressions like the *Summa Theologica* of Saint Thomas Aquinas, in works of art, in painting, sculpture, and architecture, in the Romanesque, the Gothic, the Baroque, in the extraordinary art of the Renaissance, in the statues of the prophets by Aleijadinho, in literary works like the *Divine Comedy* of Dante, in the music of Bach and Father José Mauricio, in the cathedrals in Chartres, Paris, and Brasilia, and in monuments like the Christ of Corcovado and the sumptuous edifice of the Vatican itself. All these works show the historic power of the incarnation.

But its highest expression takes place in the poor and oppressed with whom Jesus identified. They are the privileged ones of Jesus, the first addressees of his message and his love. Where the poor are, there is Jesus. Next, Jesus becomes present in those followers who go to live among the poor and oppressed, becoming one of them, bearing with them the passion of Jesus, which cries out for resurrection. They suffer, are misunderstood, jailed as subversives, tortured for being revolutionaries, and murdered as enemies of the people and of religion. It is they who most incarnate the Son in the form of suffering servant and persecuted prophet. In becoming incarnate, the Son Jesus also limited himself to that culture, to that ecological space, to the possibilities of that language, and to the provincial character of his people. Although limited, he was not imprisoned in those constraints, for the Christic power that radiated out from him broke all barriers and found other routes in history, as it found and will keep finding, until one day, which only Mystery will know, when He, Jesus the Son, will break forth in his full revelation. And we will be like him and be part of his human and cosmic community.

3.   The era of the Father/Joseph

It is the Father who most represents Mystery in itself. The one who ever withdraws: "No one has ever seen God. It is God the only Son, who is close to the Father's heart, who has made him known" (Jn 1:18; Jn 6:46; 1 Tim 6:16; 1 Jn 4:12). And it is through the Father that God is shown as Mystery to himself, accordingly, pregnant with future, with promises, with possibility of self-communication. The Father does not exist without the Son. The Breath (as the word itself suggests), the Spirit, represents the relationship between Father and Son. The Father is Father not primarily by being creator but by being eternally, before creation, the Father of the Son. If there were no Son, there would be no Father. Therefore, it is the Son who draws the Father out of his unfathomable Mystery and makes him known: "No one knows the Father except the Son" (Mt 11:27; Lk 10:22). This was the great work of Jesus, who, in feeling himself to be Son, discovers God not merely as creator of heaven and earth, but as Father of the Son and Father of unparalleled goodness and intimacy: *Abba*. The mutual communion is so complete that Jesus could confess: "I and the Father are one" (Jn 10:30). But the Son is never alone. The other sons and daughters of the Father break in with the Son. Thus, he is "the first among many brothers and sisters" (Rom 8:29). This fatherhood extends through the universe as mysterious loving Energy that is ever there, projecting new beings, sustaining each creature, and silently underlying all processes.

The Father is the prototype of love, mercy, welcome to the prodigal son, and care for the little ones. Jesus did not elaborate any doctrine on the Father. He lived his experience of being Son of the Father, the Father who thereby came close to the fallen and the lost in order to offer them the joy of his reign and of salvation. In justifying a miracle on the Sabbath, Jesus reveals his stance of close relationship with the Father: "My Father works until now and I also work" (Jn 5:17). This Father is so good to all his creatures that he displays motherly characteristics. The Father of Jesus is Mother of infinite kindness and mercy. That is why in the experience of Jesus, God can also be invoked as Mother, for he has all the characteristics of mothers who care for, love to the end, and are capable of dying for their sons and daughters. The God of Jesus is a motherly Father and a fatherly Mother.

The affirmation of the source fatherhood that gives rise to the sonship of all in the Son makes us discover universal kinship and communion among all. If we abandon this trinitarian sonship and daughterhood and the equality of all sons and daughters, we will fall ineluctably into the figure of the patriarchal Father, creator of all, who remains sole and unique, a conception that has been historically manipulated to provide a basis for the authoritarianism, paternalism, and machismo that have caused and are still causing so much evil to humankind. Jesus rightly says: "And call no one your father on earth, for you have one Father—the one in heaven" (Mt 23:9). The only religion of Father is one that, along with the Son, includes the sons and daughters composing the great family of equals, through the cohesion and harmony aroused by the Spirit.

Everything that has to do with fatherhood in the history of life, whether human or nonhuman, is connected to the Father. Everything concerned with care, providence, and the course of evolution has an essential relationship with the Father. But also everything that encloses Mystery that defies our understanding and that leads us to move from horizon to horizon while knowing never ceases, and Mystery remains impenetrable Mystery, is a way in which the Father-Mystery lets himself be discerned in history. His absence directs us to his mysterious presence.

It is proper to the work of the Father as absolute Mystery to be lived without being consciously named. He is the hidden source of all currents. They lead back to the origin, even though it is always hidden and invisible in them. The *ignotus Deus* of the religions is the Father himself under a thousand different names but accepted and adored as the mysterious, loving, and originating Ultimate Reality. It is proper to the work of the Father to arouse in us the insatiable desire of a Welcoming Womb, in which all absurdities are clarified, all fears disappear, and all tenderness is lived as supreme happiness and endless peace.

Finally, it falls to the era of the Father to carry out the work of the Son, to finally set up, in the inspiration of the Spirit, the reign that will then be the reign of the Trinity. This reign has begun in the person of Jesus and continues in the realization of the justice of the poor and oppressed with the courage and resilience that the Holy Spirit ever arouses. From mysterious Father, the Father becomes the kind sponsor of the humble and abandoned. He becomes most present in those whose sonship and daughterhood is most denied. Their sonship and daughterhood represent a challenge to the Father himself to show them all his love, compassion, and mercy as he did toward those enslaved in Egypt.

In a hardworking silent man with calloused hands, called just, since everything he did was well done, so much so that he stood out in the community, an exemplary father who brought his son into the family piety and into the great traditions of the fathers of the faith, who shared life with Mary and loved her, who faced with her the mortal threats to the child, and who went into exile with her and lived the everyday life of every pious Jewish family, Joseph, the Father found the support that could accept and bear his full presence. The Father communicated himself completely to Joseph. He became Joseph. Joseph, in his humility, without understanding anything but fully committed to the designs of the Mystery, welcomed the Father into himself, became Father personified. The Father put aside his transcendence, abandoned his mysteriousness, and with the Son and the Spirit wanted to enter into human and cosmic history in order to emerge out of and into it. The divine family now merges with the human family, while the differences of nature of each of the persons is maintained. But the entire Trinity-God finally heard the plea of all hearts and of all the ages to be able to feel and live together with the First and Last Reality: God, reveal your face, show yourself as you are, as love, communion, and compassion.

3.

Christianity and Jesus

1.   A root experience: The end is near

I take for granted critical knowledge of the biblical sources, the theologies underlying the Gospels as we have them, and devotion and reflection for over two thousand years, in order to respond to the following inquiries: What did Jesus really intend when he moved among us? Who was he, ultimately? Why has he taken on the historic importance that he has?

First, as with all events, we need to situate Jesus within cosmogenic, biogenic, and historic time. He is fruit of all that came before him. He is one of its best flowerings, although he did not present himself that way and was not even aware of it.

Jesus in cosmogenic, biogenic, and historic time

First, Jesus was a child of cosmic history, for in it are present all the energies and physical-chemical elements present in all things, from the galaxy clusters, the most distant stars, the sun and the earth, to our own body. The iron that ran in his veins, the calcium and phosphorus that strengthened his bones and nerves, the nitrogen that assured his growth, the 65 percent oxygen and 18 percent carbon that made up his bodily reality, and other physical-chemical elements mean that Jesus is really a cosmic being.

Since the universe has not only exteriority but also interiority and subjectivity the outgrowth of the network of relationships of all with all, and of what has been learned, and of the information emerging therefrom that continues to accumulate, we can say that dwelling in the psychic depths of Jesus are the most primitive movements of the cosmic, mineral, vegetable, animal, and human unconscious, the most archaic dreams, the most deep-seated passions, the deepest archetypes, and the most ancestral symbols. Like all humans, Jesus was also an African, because it was in Africa that the human species and consciousness broke out.

In a word, Jesus was also a product of the great initial explosion, the Big Bang, with the developments that ensued. And in recent history his roots are in the Milky Way, his home in the solar system, his cradle on the Planet Earth, his geographical location in Palestine, and his dwelling in Nazareth. Like any other human being, he is a child of the cosmos and of the earth.

Like other human beings, Jesus is mammal, of the order of primates, of the family of hominids, of the genus *homo,* of the species *sapiens.* His body is a machine of fifty trillion cells, controlled and procreated by a genetic system that has been built up over the course of a long natural evolution, going back 3.8 million years, the time when life emerged; the brain with which he thought having over fifty billion neurons that make a hundred trillion connections; the mouth with which he spoke, the hand with which he touched, his biological organs all marked by a most sophisticated evolutionary process until they reached where they are now.

He is likewise son of the history of humankind, as the Gospels express in their manner through the genealogies, connecting Jesus to Adam (Luke) with all the subjectivity and spirituality that characterizes human life. He is son of Abraham (Matthew), member of the Hebrew people, with its singular experience of God, a people bearing dreams and utopias coming to maturity in the religious and political experiences of slavery in Egypt and captivity in Babylon, a people of prophets, martyrs, and poets, among the greatest of all humankind.

Finally, Jesus is son of Miriam, adopted by her husband, Joseph, both representing the Jewish culture of their time. He thought and acted with the resources offered him by his culture. Even the fact that he is the incarnation of the Son of the Father does not nullify his human condition. On the contrary, it reinforces it, for the Council of Chalcedon (451), which made this conviction official doctrine, holds that Jesus was always and in everything truly human, like any other man, and that his relationship with the Father was never broken.

Jesus is a man, not a woman. As a man he bears the cumulative ever-tense and often conflictive experiences of the encounter of genders, with the singular qualities of the man, with a proper way of feeling, thinking, and speaking the world, along with its limitations. Being a man he carries within himself his feminine dimension, a constitutive reality of every human being, along with the masculine dimension. This feminine dimension is shown by the way he understands *Abba*-God with a mother's features; by the spiritual sense he confers on everything he does; by concern for those who suffer; by kindness toward children; by love and friendship for Martha, Mary, and Lazarus; and by sensitivity to the lily in the field and to the vine. The presence of these two energies allowed him a more comprehensive and complete experience of what the human being is, man and woman, different but in permanent relationship of reciprocity, complementarity, and dialectical tension.

All these layers of reality, from the cosmic to the Hebraic and familial, are present and inter-retro-connected in Jesus. Without them or outside of them he would not be concrete, the one who traveled the dusty roads of Palestine, proclaiming a new state of awareness, that we really all are sons and daughters, and workers in a new reign built on justice out of the poor and marginalized, a reign of unconditional love, universal kinship, compassion, unlimited forgiveness, and lasting peace. Like many peasants and artisans similar to him, Jesus lived in radical but nonviolent resistance to the urban development of Herod Antipas and to Rome's rural commercialism in lower Galilee, one of the most fertile areas in the world at this time. The overall context in which Jesus lived was one of fierce opposition by the Jewish homeland against Greek cultural internationalism and Roman military imperialism.

Jesus, a man of his time: An apocalyptic?

In terms of his worldview Jesus was an apocalyptic. This apocalyptic vision was typical of many in his time. It has to do with a truth that is hidden but is slowly being revealed, that we are nearing a dramatic end to the present order that will open space to the glad tidings of the emergence of a new configuration brought in by God himself, called the reign of God. It will be the "Day of the Lord," as was said in apocalyptic circles.

Like Jesus, the apocalyptics interpreted the world as follows: The world has reached such a point of degradation that its end is near, but God has decided to intervene for liberation, abolishing all evil, and inaugurating the reign of God, of justice, love, and perpetual peace. And he will do it through a unique figure, the liberating Messiah together with his community. His action will take place in a highly dramatic setting, with clashes between peoples, earthquakes, convulsion in the heavens, and primarily with temptations for the good and the elect. The situation is one of urgency, for the in-breaking may occur by surprise and at any time—that is why one must be prepared—but it will be a joy for all the people (Lk 2:18). Jesus assumed this worldview; that is the starting point for explaining the radical and urgent character of his preaching and his practice.

Jesus did not preach the church but the reign of God. His intention was directed at humankind and was not restricted to a portion of it, to Judaism or to the church. He did not have in mind a new religion but a new man, a new woman, a new heaven, and a new earth. Everything would be subjected to the politics of God for his creation, translated as the incipient presence of the reign of God. This reign is in ongoing confrontation with the empire, which is the power of the negative, the current situation of the world and of creation, subjected to the energies of oppression, rejection, sin, and death. Both are in constant conflict, and Jesus feels involved in it.

A metaphor: A destructive meteor is approaching

In order to make concrete the apocalyptic vision, to understand its internal logic, its urgent character and the excitement that it caused, let us give an example, one that could be experienced in our own time, marked by convulsions of nature and threats of extermination of species and of human civilization itself.

Let us imagine the following scenario, which has happened countless times in the history of the earth: Astronomers in various parts of the world clearly detect a powerful meteor that is rapidly heading toward the earth, say *Atrophis 2036*, or any other. It is so large that it may devastate the biosphere and jeopardize the future of humankind. The last one, which was huge in proportion, occurred sixty-five million years ago, when a meteor approximately six miles in diameter crashed into the Caribbean causing a true environmental Armageddon. For many dozens of years the sun was darkened and the climates of the earth changed completely. The dinosaurs, who reigned unchallenged over the earth for 133 million years, were quickly wiped out.

When facing such an extreme situation, in practice there is nothing to do but wait and prepare for the collective catastrophe. The scientific community calculates that very soon the asteroid will fall incandescent into earth's atmosphere. The consequences are unpredictable, but they will be devastating and horrifying in any case. It may impossible for us to survive on earth; we may all be destroyed.

Creative destruction: The reign begins

What stance are we to take? Give up hope? Wait for a divine miracle at the last minute? Isn't the earth system open, so can't it prepare a surprise for us out of the Foundation Energy of the universe? Can't God utilize the unavoidable destruction to usher in a new order, but one that will be inclusive and will benefit all? Or step in, eliminate the empire and its wrongdoing, and assure a happy ending for his creation?

We can imagine the many possible reactions of human beings to this terminal reality. Some despair, and out of fear of dying kill themselves. Some want to live it up, as in the time of Noah, and will say, "Let us eat and drink for tomorrow we shall die" (1 Cor 15:32). Some are unbelievers and continue as if nothing were happening, saying that all this is no more than a joke that the scientific community has played on humankind, and they keep making plans for the future, gambling on the stock exchange, investing in huge enterprises, doing business, and piling up wealth. Some are preachers of conversion and penitence like John the Baptist, for along with mass death, they see the harsh judgment of God, who will punish the evil and reward the good. Finally, some like Jesus take seriously the imminence of the end, but they interpret it as good news; this crashing meteor will mean that "the time of waiting is over, the reign is drawing near, let us change our life and believe in this good news" (cf. Mk 1:15).

Therefore, the end is inevitable but does not have to be catastrophic. Despite the abomination of desolation, the occasion appears to be propitious for God, finally, to destroy the empire of evil and to usher in the new heavens and new earth, his definitive reign. But, beware! We only have this short time to prepare ourselves and thus to go not toward death but to meet the Source of life, toward the reign that comes from the heavens, brought by God, though the fall of a meteor, which annihilates the old humanity.

Such is the mental world of Jesus, the psychological and cultural context of his activity, in the framework of the apocalyptic vision. Everything is urgent. Radical changes are imminent. And according to Jesus, they will be good, even wonderful. Finally the ancestral dreams of a new world and the visions of a new humanity, open and faithful to God, of a society of brotherly and sisterly feeling, within a reconciled universe, are going to blossom. The time of waiting is over. At last!

What is positive in the apocalyptic vision?

What matters, therefore, isn't recognizing the fact that Jesus took on the apocalyptic vision as he could have taken on any other vision also in fashion in his time. What is decisive is grasping the experience that he elaborated within this type of vision and this psychosocial context. What meaning did he confer on it? He translated this experience in the form of a luminous message and a generous ethical practice that still affects us today. This experience gave rise to the Jesus movement, which has never ceased in history. From it emerged communities and churches that have nourished the various spiritual paths they believe are within the legacy of Jesus.

This root experience of Jesus was expressed in (1) a practice, (2) a message, (3) an ethic, (4) a fate, and (5) a verification. All the texts of the Second Testament, especially the four Gospels, and all the subsequent expressions, varying in their intellectual, artistic, and ethical nature, are attempts at understanding, interpreting, and translating this root experience of Jesus.

2.   A dream: The reign of God

The dream is what gives meaning to the life of a person and a community. The dream is what is most decisive in life. The materials we are all made of are personal and common dreams; that is why the dream is an essential part of human reality. That reality has a factual, concrete, always closed side, and another side that is virtual, possible, and ever open. The factual is a dream that is achieved. The dream is that which cannot yet happen and that is struggling to break through and make history. What moves us are dreams, that which is not yet but that can and will be. Jesus was consumed by a great dream: the reign of God. He did not preach himself, or the church, or even God as such. He proclaimed: "The time of waiting is over. The reign of God is approaching. Change your life. Believe in this good news" (Mk 1:15). In this regard he is different from John the Baptist, whose disciple he may have been, who probably spent time in the caves of the Essenes in Qumran, next to the Dead Sea, rigorous ascetics with a high morality and values linked to love and forgiveness. John proclaimed the impending judgment and necessary conversion. Jesus, on the contrary, felt that that was not where his path went; he proclaimed the joy of the reign that is now under way and that is going to be brought about insofar as his hearers accept it and are converted.

The expression "reign of God" occurs 122 times in the Gospels and 90 times on Jesus' lips, thereby showing that it sums up his dream. The dream responds to the deepest expectations of human seeking. All suffer from divisions and hatreds, and yearn for union and peace; they are afflicted by the weight of human malice, bearing the heavy load of daily work, the necessary price of survival; they want to participate in a harmonious shared life, fear illness, and flee death; they experience rebellious nature and yearn to see it calm and friendly to life; they seek a healthy existence and dream of a happy life; they want to be right with God and feel him in everyday life. God always gives himself but also withdraws. And that is painful. When will he show his blessed face? Dreams are unlimited. Each stage of achievement is the platform for a new beginning. The dream never dies.

The reign of God seeks to respond to these basic questions with which people are always faced. Specifically, Jesus lived under two kinds of oppression that cried out for his dream to be realized: an *external* oppression, the occupation of the Promised Land by the military forces of the Roman Empire, with an emperor who demanded that he be worshiped as God. The Jews experienced this as shocking, and it aroused the dream of a divine intervention to redeem the sacredness of the land of the patriarchs. Some, even among the apostles, believed that Jesus could bring about this kind of political liberation. That was why he was seen as a political subversive (Lk 23:2, 14), which may have led to a conflict with the Romans. There was another *internal* oppression: the prevalence of a legalistic religion that distanced God from the world and placed him in the meshes of myriad norms and rituals. Jesus proposes the reign of God over against the empire of Caesar. It was a subversive and dangerous political act. As opposed to the religion of law, Jesus proposes the religion of love and mercy. That proposal made Jesus a heretic and embroiled him in a religious conflict with the guardians of the religious order. These two fronts of tension, as a subversive and heretic, accompanied Jesus throughout his life and marked his path to the point of becoming unsustainable. The solution was that he was condemned to death for political (Romans) and religious (Pharisees and priestly caste) reasons.

By its dream nature, reign of God is the most all-encompassing representation possible. It represents God's politics in his creation. It is an absolute, total, and radical revolution. It is going to change the foundations of personal, community, earthly, and cosmic reality. God has decided to begin a process of rescuing his creation and leading it to its fulfillment. Like any dream it has an aspect of *presence*. otherwise it would be daydream and fantasy: "The reign has drawn near" (Mk 1:14), "the reign has come to you" (Lk 17:21), "the reign of God is within you" (Lk 17:21). The reign is indeed there in the world, in reality, in life, and so it represents a summons to all to pay attention and listen in order to grasp it and hear it. What are called miracles should be understood as signs that the reign is under way and is manifest in history (Lk 11:20; Mt 11:3, 5). On the other hand, the reign has a *future* dimension. Jesus teaches to pray: "thy kingdom come." He proclaims a process that is taking place in history insofar as people are accepting this transformation. It is like a seed thrown into the earth (Mk 4:26), like a grain of mustard (Mt 13:31), like leaven in dough (Mt 13:22). These metaphors point toward a concrete presence and toward a magnificent future promise. In the seed is the plant of tomorrow; in the grain of mustard is concealed a large future tree. In the handful of leaven is the bounteous bread to be baked. That is, the littleness conceals the greatness of an indomitable power. In the beginning is present the end, which is slowly taking shape.

The reign of God is not a territory, limited to the space of Palestine, but a new order of things: the last will be first, the little ones will be great; the lowly will be the masters, the sick will be healed; the deaf will hear, the oppressed will be liberated; those scattered will be reunited, suffering will disappear, mourning will be no more; death will be overcome, and the dead will arise. This program is present in his first public appearance in the synagogue of Nazareth (Lk 4:18–19). God will be experienced as Father of infinite mercy. The intimacy is such that he is called *Abba,* beloved Papa.

The reign is not just *spiritual.* It encompasses all creation, and so it heals persons, feeds the hungry, halts winds, and calms the stormy sea (Mk 4:29). It forgives sins and promises grace and redemption to all, starting with those farthest away and most lost. It always preserves a character of universality and totality. No one is beyond the scope of the reign. Nothing is greater than it.

The reign of God cannot be *split off* as though it were part of something larger. It cannot be reduced to the three kinds of power presented as temptations to which Jesus was subjected (Mk 1:12ff.; Mt 4:11; Lk 4:1–13): *prophetic* power, which changes stones into bread; *priestly* power, which seeks to change the world from the temple and moral reform; or *political* power, which dominates peoples and territories, and subjects all to a single order. Jesus rejects these three kinds of power as diabolical temptations. The road chosen is that of the servant leader, the persecuted prophet, and suffering servant announced by the prophet Isaiah (Is 53).

The reign is not *of* this world but *in* this world. Interrogated by Pilate whether he is king, Jesus replies: "My reign is not *of this* world" (Jn 18:36). Indeed, his origin is not to be found in this world but in God. He begins to be fulfilled in *this* world. This dream of the reign of God that inhabited Jesus' life made him leave his parental home, to the point of being considered crazy by his relatives (Mk 3:21), and travel through villages and cities, proclaiming the joy of this advent of God into his creation.

This radical dream, which demanded deep transformations, ran into harsh resistance from those upholding the established order of the time and brought down on Jesus curses, persecutions, and eventually a political and religious condemnation. That was indeed what happened with Jesus. But he took his dream to the end, to the point of undergoing the hell of the absence of God on the cross (Mk 15:34) and sense of utter failure. However, the dream never dies. The life of Jesus, like a tree, was cut off at the top, its branches were chopped off, and its trunk torn up by the roots, but the seed remained, with all the drive that it contains. Out of the seed come the roots, the trunk springs forth, the branches emerge, the crown takes shape, the leaves tremble, the flowers smile, and the fruits are produced. There stands the entire tree. This transformation took place in Jesus by his life, which broke the limits of death by resurrection. Something of the dream, of the reign that has partly arrived, is achieved there.

3. A practice: Liberation

The dream is only true when it is translated into practice. It begins to be achieved with those who are last, those who are most oppressed and marginalized. Jesus comes forth as their liberator. In first place are the poor, called blessed (Mk 6:20), the privileged in the reign of God. This comes from the essence of God who, being life, feels attracted to those who have least life, because they are denied life by oppression. They are victims, the impoverished. No one is for them, they are made invisible, that is why God takes their side, comes to liberate them, and they are the first beneficiaries of the new order that is the reign of God. Then come those who are marginalized for any reason: sickness, blindness, or paralysis, or for any sort of discrimination, such as women, prostitutes, the Samaritan heretic, the publican, functionary of the empire, the Roman official, the pagan Syro-Phoenician woman, those regarded as public sinners. He eats with them, a sign that grace and intimacy with the Father also extends to them. Because of this scandalous audacity, they call him a "glutton, drinker, and friend of disreputable people" (Mt 11:19; Lk 7:34).

Full liberation is achieved in the practice of unconditional love as the organizing principle of relations among persons. Love does not divide, it unites. Even love for God goes by way of love for neighbor (Mt 23:27–40). For Jesus, neighbor means the one I come close to. And I should come close to all, but especially those that no one wants to come close to, the marginalized, the poor, the sick, and the disreputable. For Jesus, loving the neighbor means especially loving these last. "Loving those who love us, what is special about that? The evil also love those who love them" (Lk 6:32). Love for the invisible and the despised reveals the uniqueness of the love desired by Jesus, almost never practiced by Christians and the churches. In fact, unconditional love is a single movement toward the other and toward God. Jesus wants everyone to love *Abba*-Father as he has loved him, with utter trust and intimacy. Whoever has this love has everything because God himself is love (1 Jn 4:8).

But, for Jesus, love must be clothed with a quality that makes it characteristic. Love has to be merciful. Only someone who is imbued with mercy can understand and live the call of Jesus: "Love your enemies, do good to those who hate you, speak well of those who curse you, and pray for those who slander you" (Lk 6:27–28). To live this dimension of love is to be free. Offense, humiliation, and violence received keep us imprisoned in bitterness, and often with a spirit of revenge. Forgiveness frees us from these bonds, makes us fully free. Free to love. The father forgives the prodigal son (Lk 15:11–32) without demanding anything of him for his debauchery. It is not enough to be good like the obedient and faithful son who stayed home, the only one who is criticized. One must be merciful, which he was not. That is the supreme freedom: to break the chains that keep us enclosed in the past that we have suffered, and to transcend it toward the reign of freedom and autonomy. This is the work of mercy and forgiveness. Mercy is an essential quality of God: "He is kind to the ungrateful and wicked; be merciful as the Father is merciful" (Lk 6:36). Without mercy we would lose an essential dimension of the experience of Jesus toward his *Abba*-Father, and we would be deprived of this fundamental characteristic of God. The legalists, the moralists, the authoritarians, so much a part of conservative Christian circles and in certain groups in society and civic and religious institutions, must face up to this merciful dimension of Jesus.

In the name of love he relativizes traditions, frees from oppressive laws—"the Sabbath was made for man, not man for the Sabbath" (Mt 2:27)—and subjects all power structures to rigorous critique. They cannot be for oppression, but rather must be places for exercising freedom and functions of pure service: "Whoever wants to be first must be last" (Mk 9:35).

Practice toward God goes not by way of official ritual, but by love, mercy, sense of justice, and trusting surrender to him who cares for every hair on one's head (Lk 21:18). It accepts all with no distinctions, for that is God's merciful attitude, assumed by Jesus who said: "Anyone who comes to me I will not turn away" (Jn 6:37). It may be a fearful theologian like Nicodemus, who seeks him in the dead of night, a Samaritan woman alongside the well, a blind man who cries out to him to be healed, or a desperate woman who asks him to raise up her little daughter who has just died. He attends to all without distinction. He is a being-for-others. This sentence, "Anyone who comes to me I will not turn away," expresses one of the most beautiful and emblematic of the practices of Jesus.

Everyone realizes that there is a confrontation between the empire of Caesar to which all must submit and worship as "god" and the reign of God, which assumes the absolute sovereignty of God over creation and over history. When he says, "Give to Caesar what is Caesar's and to God what is God's," he is responding to a theological demand that is at the same time political. The question is: Must Caesar be adored as god? He replies: Give Caesar what is Caesar's, for he is just a man, not a god; since he is just a man don't give him adoration, which is wrong and blasphemous. But give God what is God's, that is, adoration and praise. He thereby denies the divine character of Caesar, which constitutes a crime of *lèse majesté*.

Where legalism gives way to liberty, where shared life replaces discrimination, where love prevails over self-interest, where trust overcomes fear, where acceptance of the proposal for a new life replaces traditions, the reign begins to be established. It is only a beginning, something real and new that has gotten under way. It has an impact and causes joy. But it also causes astonishment because entrance into the reign is not automatic. Entry is only through change of life. Is everyone ready for this transformation of attitudes? A decision is required, a deed that creates a split between what was and what ought to be. There begins a *crisis,* a word that Saint John uses seventeen times in his Gospel, in the sense of a break and a decision that affects everyone: the people, the religious authorities, his followers, and even the disciples who threaten to leave him (Jn 6:67). Jesus is aware of the hardness of heart of the pious Pharisees and of the inconstancy of those closest to him. Accusations that he is a false prophet (Mt 27:62), possessed (Mk 3:22), crazy (Mk 3:24), subversive (Lk 23:2, 13), heretical (Jn 8:48), and the like pile up. He realizes that they want to wipe him out. He does not set out to seek death. He hides and even takes refuge in the city of Ephraim (Jn 11:54), where his enemies cannot legally get at him. Even that does not discourage him. He continues to trust in the capacity of people to open themselves and accept the great liberating dream. The time is short and the catastrophic meteor is drawing near. What matters is alerting and inviting people to what is new and about to break in.

The reign is built up against the empire of oppression; hence, its conflictive nature from start to finish. As resistance and confrontation increase, Jesus slowly realizes that the reign that is barely beginning with him may fail. This makes him assume all the more decisively the path of the suffering servant and persecuted prophet. In a stance of absolute greatness of soul, he takes on himself the rejection, the "sins" of others, in order to draw on divine mercy so that no one will be excluded from the reign. Since they were not reached by love, they will be by forgiveness. If they have not been reached by love, they will be by mercy and the offer of forgiveness.

Slowly, but clearly, Jesus realizes that the path of suffering has been reserved for him by the Father. It will not be easy to accept this painful way of the cross. That is where Jesus' faith comes in, and he proves to be a man of faith (Heb 12:2), which leads him to total surrender and unlimited confidence. His cry of abandonment and despair on the height of the cross (Mk 15:34) attests to the depth of Jesus' aloneness. Hope is threatened, and with it the reality of the dream and of the liberation connected to it. But ultimately, with no other support and completely emptied and freed of himself, he surrenders to the nameless Mystery. He makes his way into the reign of terrifying and frightful inner darkness of which the mystics speak. Love of God and humankind demand this *kenosis,* this liberation from himself, from his convictions, from his awareness of being the initiator of the reign. It is the nature of the dream to be ever resurrected. Only what is dies; what is not yet cannot die. What can be, what is virtual and possible, like the dream of the reign and of a creation finally liberated and taken to its fullness, never dies. It always continues as the dream of the best, dream of Jesus and of all, from "Abel, the just one, to the last of the elect," as the fathers at Vatican II wrote (*Lumen Gentium*, no. 2).

4. A message: Our Father and our bread

What is the core of Jesus' message, formulated in the patterns of apocalyptic culture? This message underlies all the writings in the First Testament. In them we find attempts at understanding, at adaptation and translation of this message in contexts that are no longer apocalyptic thirty or forty years after the execution of Jesus, when the movement of his followers and the widely varying communities that preserved in their own manner the memory of the deeds of Jesus had emerged. This memory was worked over by the religious concerns and theologies proper to the communities that underlie the Gospels of Mark, Matthew, Luke, and John. They obscure the original message of Jesus more than they clarify it. The true figure of his person ends up being hidden in excessive "clothing." Even so, within that tangle of texts we can identify its unquestionable core thrust. This obviously entails rigorous exegetical and critical study that we cannot demonstrate here, but it is presupposed and is found in my various writings in Christology. Surprisingly, we find it in the prayer of the Our Father. Why is it there? Because that is precisely where Jesus' original intention is hidden, rather than in any other formulation. It came from his own lips. That is why we call it the *ipsissima vox Jesu,* the very voice of Jesus. What are the criteria for making this assumption that has such serious consequences?

The reasons are simple. In the Our Father we find nothing of what is important for the church that came afterward: Jesus as Savior, his death and resurrection, the church, the creed, the sacraments, the Eucharist, and dogmas. Nothing is said about this. For Jesus, this isn't important. What is important and essential is *Abba*-God and God's reign, human beings and their needs. Even more concisely, it is about Our Father and our bread[1] in the arc of the dream of God's reign. This is Jesus' message in a nutshell. If we are asked what Jesus wanted, we should reply that he wanted to bring the reign of God, that we should feel God as close, Father and Mother of kindness *(Abba),* and that we should seek our bread. Everything else is commentary.

When the disciples ask Jesus, "Lord, teach us to pray (cf. Lk 11:1), they are not seeking a method of prayer, something familiar to every Jew. This question represents a linguistic contest, well known at the time, for saying, "Jesus, give us a summary of your teaching." "What is the logo of your teaching?" We know that the various religious groups of the time were distinguished by short prayer formulas that summed up their respective doctrines and gave them identity and internal cohesion. The same thing happens with Jesus. The Our Father reveals the root experience of Jesus and presents us with his *ipsissima intentio,* that is, his truest intention. This is a "Jesuanic" text, that is, a text that came directly from the lips of the Jesus of history.

Thus, the Our Father is in keeping with the three fundamental and constant hungers of human beings: The hunger to encounter someone good who embraces them and means life, joy, and acceptance; this someone is the kind "Papa" *(Abba).* The second hunger is the infinite hunger that is never satisfied, the grand dream of a full meaning for life, for history, and for the universe; it comes under the name of reign of God. The third hunger that is satisfied, but without which we do not live, is our bread. Without this material basis there is no point in speaking of our Father or of the reign of God, for a corpse does not call on our Father or expect the reign.

We can never forget this nutshell. It cannot be replaced by doctrines, dogmas, rituals, and traditions. There we would be departing from the root intention of Jesus; the oldest Christian tradition intuited that when facing the Our Father we were standing before something that belongs to the secret and the Mystery of Jesus. That

---

[1] *Translator's note:* A wordplay in Portuguese: *pai,* "father," and *pão,* "bread."

is why this prayer belonged to the discipline of what was hidden; that is, it was taught only to initiates who had been baptized and confirmed. Tertullian (d. 225), the greatest lay theologian of the early church, says emphatically that the Our Father is the *breviarum totius evangelii,* the summary of the whole gospel.

In view of its importance, we are going to transcribe in parallel columns the two versions that we find in the gospels of Luke (11:2–4) and Matthew (6:9–13).

Matthew	Luke
Our Father, you who are in the heavens, hallowed be your name;	Father, hallowed be your name;
may your reign come to us, may your will be done on earth as in heaven.	may your reign come.
Give us our daily bread today,	Give us each day the necessary bread;
Forgive us our debts as we forgive our debtors,	forgive us our sins, for we also forgive all who have offended us,
and do not let us fall into temptation,	and do not put us to the test.
but deliver us from evil.	

As is clear, the two versions are different in form but substantially the same in content. The difference is due to the fact that the prayer of Jesus was passed on and assimilated in the various early Christian communities. For the letter was less important than the spirit; that spirit is concentrated in this unbreakable Our Father/ our bread union, in the arc of the reign of God, attested in both versions.

Out of historiographical concern, although not so important to us, we may ask: Which of the two versions is the original, the one that came from Jesus' lips? Luke, shorter, contains everything that is present more expansively in Matthew. Scholars assure us that when a shorter formula is found wholly contained in the longer one, it is the shorter one that ought to be considered closer to the original. Hence, it would be that of Saint Luke. Since both say fundamentally the same thing, in order to facilitate our reflection, we are going to lean toward Saint Matthew's version, because his development allows for better seizing of the primary intention of Jesus.

"Our Father, you who are in the heavens." One thing is utterly certain historically: Jesus always called his God *Abba*, which is a word taken from children's vocabulary, a diminutive indicating intimacy. It means *my dear Papa.* This expression occurs 170 times on Jesus' lips. The Second Testament preserves this expression, *Abba*, in Jesus' dialect, Aramaic. It thereby wishes to keep the occurrence of this absolutely singular state of awareness (cf. Rom 8:15; Gal 4:6): the fact that he called God his beloved Papa.

We evoke the authority of one of the greatest scholars of the expression *Abba*, the German, Joachim Jeremias. This is how he sums up its unprecedented meaning: "Jesus addresses God like a little child to his father, with the same intimate simplicity, the same trusting abandonment." For God is not an implacable judge of the moralizers, nor a terrifying abyss of the philosophers, nor an inscrutable energy of the astrophysicists toward which we fall silent in reverence. He undoubtedly has the characteristics of nameless formless Mystery. But here he emerges as an outpouring of love and compassion because "he knows our nature and remembers that we are dust" (Ps 103:13–14), in the context of an experience of warm tenderness and emotional intimacy as pious people and the mystics of all ages experience him. Son means more than a causal relationship (every son proceeds biologically from the parents), it is a personal relationship. The son is all the more son insofar as he cultivates the space of intimacy and trusting surrender to the father.

God is *Abba*-Father because he cares for his sons and daughters, his affection rests on each of them, he knows the name that his love invented for each of them, he knows their needs, he feels their least heartbeat, he does not let a single hair of their head fall without knowing about it (Lk 21:18), he causes the sun to rise on them and the rain to fall on their heads, even when they are ungrateful and evil (cf. Lk 6:35), and he gathers them under his protection as a hen does her chicks (Mt 23:37). This *Abba*-Father shows motherly features, for he is all about care, love, and mercy, as shown in forgiveness to the prodigal son (Lk 15:11–32), in anxiety to find the lost coin (Lk 15:8–10), in the untiring search for the runaway sheep (Mt 18:12ff.; Lk 15:4). This *Abba*-Father is motherly, and this Mother is fatherly. This is the God of Jesus' root experience, God-Father-and-Mother of infinite goodness and mercy, or simply *Abba*.

One who calls God "my dear Papa" or "my dear Mama" feels that he is their beloved son. *Father* and *Son* are correlative terms. There is no Father without son or son without Father. *Abba* contains the inner secret of Jesus, his hidden Mystery. We can say that this awareness of being Son of an *Abba*-God has not emerged without long preparation. I would say that it was slowly emerging in the process of cosmogenesis, biogenesis, and anthropogenesis, creating the conditions of complexity and interiority of matter and life, until it burst forth consciously in Jesus. Something unique and singular has happened on our earth, in our solar system, perhaps in our galaxy and in the universe: the emergence of the Son from within the process of evolution, on the basis of awareness of *Abba*-Father. Jesus himself confirms it: "No one knows the Father except the Son and he to whom he wished to reveal it" (Mt 11:27).

Stated in cosmogenic terms it means this: It wasn't simply Jesus who developed this experience of fatherhood/motherhood/sonship, with him as sole subject. The subject is the universe in genesis. This experience was always in preparation. The Originating Source, that intelligent and loving, underlying ineffable Energy was at work in the forces guiding the universe, permeating every stage of evolution, was breaking forth in all living beings, creating interiority and subjectivity in them, and especially was fostering the spirit of human beings until it was transformed into conscious content: perceiving God as *Abba* and as himself as his Son. This happened in the man Jesus of Nazareth, born from a people, the least of all peoples (Dt 7:7), an inhabitant of an insignificant region of the Roman Empire, Galilee, from a family of poor migrants, rooted in the village of Nazareth, so unknown that it is never found in any of the writings of the First Testament. In this concrete being, Mediterranean Jew, Galilean, craftsman, farmer, born under the *immensa romanae pacis maiestas* (under the immense majesty of Roman peace), there sprang forth the awareness of God as Father/ Mother of kindness and forgiveness *(Abba)*, welcoming all as his beloved and loved sons and daughters, especially the oppressed, hungry, naked, and thirsty, whom Jesus will call "my least brothers and sisters" (Mt 25:40).

"Hallowed be your name." Let's be realistic. There is an a priori point that helps us understand this plea: In the world, out of human malice and the rebellion of creation, God's name is manipulated, distorted, and trivialized by all the media, especially by religious programs on TV, most of them mediocre and unworthy of the grandeur of Jesus. What goes on there most of the time is the sin against the second commandment, taking God's name in vain. Given the calamities of the world, many find no reasons to praise God and sadly lament, like Job in the Bible; others do not withstand God's long silence in the face of injustices, especially against the innocent or against devastating earthquakes and tsunamis, against hideous crimes like the Nazi extermination camps, and they pray in silence as Benedict XVI did when he visited Auschwitz in Poland. We also, like Job, complain: "God, where were you when millions of Amerindian indigenous were wiped out by the European colonizers who killed by the cross and the sword? Why did you allow these tragedies? Why were you silent? Where are you today when you do not take pity on your sons and daughters who suffer so much? How are we to glorify the name of God?" Within this objective destitution, Jesus invites us to praise his name despite everything, especially at this time when he has decided to step in and sow the seeds of his reign.

"May your reign come to us." We have here the most ancestral sigh of the human being, deep within the ups and downs of evolution, within the contradictions of life, where good and evil mix together, and where one often has the impression that viciousness triumphs over goodness, and chaos prevails over cosmos. This is the background that gives rise to all the dreams and utopias of another possible and better world. These dreams never leave human

beings, whether sleeping or waking. In other words, we are built on the basis of the principle of desire, which indefatigably seeks to overcome the enemies of life and to initiate the reign of full freedom. The dream is located not in reason but in imagination and fantasy. There lies the principle of hope out of which spring utopias and the most generous proposals. We are utopian beings; we refuse to accept the world the way it is: we want to transform it. Prophets arise in all times and in all cultures, people moved by the inner fire who have kept alive and held high the human hope that it is not the brutality of the real that has last word but the power of that which can bring a better future. That is the root of the imperishable hope that is not so much a virtue as a driving force that always energizes us, that lifts us up when we fall and gets us back on the road.

Jesus went seeking his message in the depths of the human cry and in dreams pregnant with hope and joy. It is universal because it comes out of a universal desire. He proclaims: "The reign is coming, it is in our midst; believe in this joyful news" (Mk 1:15). There are unmistakable signs that the reign is coming near: "the blind see, the lame walk, lepers are made clean, the deaf hear, the dead rise, and the poor are the primary addressees of this newness" (cf. Lk 7:22). Therefore, the dream begins to cease being a dream and shows that it is a smiling reality.

What does the reign of God have to do with the utopian structure of the human being? It is one of its best expressions, if not the best. It represents an overthrowing of the existing order and the beginning of a new one. The primary agent is God himself, who has decided to step into the course of evolution and carry out a revolution within evolution. That is why the reign is *of God*. It begins with the least: the poor, sinners, and prostitutes. They all precede the pure and the religious in entering into the reign. All are invited: servants, crippled, marginalized (Mt 18:21–23). People will come from West and East and will sit down at the table. The most fitting metaphors for the reign are the supper, the wedding banquet, and the feast. They symbolize that the reign is the reconciliation of all things, even with nature and the universe. Reign means the joy of those freed. God comes and serves all as his sons and daughters.

But the reign is not only of God. It is also *ours*. Insofar as we open ourselves to it, we assume its dynamic and begin to inaugurate it in practice, in our daily life, in our small family world and in society: with love, injustice, forgiveness, and trusting surrender to God.

Reign has the following characteristics: It is *universal*. It includes everything: the infrastructure of human life, social relationships, cosmic dimensions, and primarily, the new experience of *Abba*-God as grace and mercy for all. The reign is also *structural,* and encompasses not only all dimensions, but goes even to their ultimate roots and revolutionizes them. It is not a mere reform of what exists but an absolute reform that creates the new. Finally, the reign is *ultimate*. By attacking the causes in their entirety and radicality, it also defines what the ultimate will of God is and the final framework of the universe. Our kind of world ends; there will come another where God will finally show himself as Lord of his previously rebellious creation. There all will find their place and their peace.

Jesus never defined the reign of God, but we can understand it on the basis of his practice and words. He attempts new relationships and a new way of being before *Abba*-God, feeling himself as Son and passing on this experience to everyone else. We have here the foundation of the dignity of each human person; no matter how humiliated and tormented, he or she is a son or daughter of God.

But this reign is not entered in any fashion whatsoever. One has to go through God's "clinic." One must change life to measure up to the dream and the utopia proclaimed. The reign has the characteristic of being *process*: it is ever coming and is established only where love prevails, justice is done, what is right is lived, and the human being converts to God and to others, to the point of love for enemies. And it is here that the drama occurs: the reign is built up against the empire of evil that permeates human history. With infinite sadness the ancient witnesses say: "He, Jesus, came to his own, and his own did not receive him" (Jn 1:11). The one who proclaims hope is rejected and physically eliminated. But the dream cannot die with him. Human beings keep nourishing hope and pleading: "May your reign come to us." "Hasten your coming and do justice against the inhabitants of earth who have spilled the blood of the just."

"May your reign come to us" is an appeal against this perverse world for a new one where God can dwell with his sons and daughters. It is a hope that does not accept the verdict of the empire of perversity and keeps hoping against all hope. The Son will be the stronger one who will overcome the strong one (Mt 3:27). The last word will not be that of death but of transfiguration of life in its fullness. This is a hope that has never disappeared, nor will it disappear from the earth. On the day when it perishes, the earth will be covered with bodies, and nature will agonize in the throes of death, and the spirits will sink into the abyss of the absurd. Christianity is a religion of hope more than of faith. Without hope it is meaningless and becomes stuck in the quagmire of the interests of the powerful of history; that is why it never tires of pleading, "May your reign come to us."

"May your will be done." This desire should be understood in the apocalyptic context in which Jesus moves about. Reality just as it is cannot be as God wills, for injustice and the muzzling of the truth abound. The reign runs into opposition; the prince of this world still has his empire. He is the great foe (2 Cor 4:4), for he drives the energies of the negative to the maximum. What is God's will? The establishment of the reign of God with all the kinds of liberation that it entails. Here the plea may be raised with urgency: "Why are you delaying, Lord? Come now and do justice for your people and your creation." God's will especially means that the human being live, that the earth be the human dwelling, that the universe end well, and that no one be under the control of the dia-bolic. The reign is *of* God but *for* the human being and for the world, especially for the little ones. That is why it must be renewed: "Whoever is not born again cannot enter into the reign of God" (Jn 3:3). Finally, doing God's will entails a component of trusting surrender, for we realize that we are vulnerable and cannot do everything. The reign has been initiated, and it is set up against the empire of perversity, which shows its capacity to raise up obstacles and destroy paths and knock down bridges. We have to observe, dumbfounded, that often

the best causes are defeated, the just person is bypassed, the sage ridiculed, and the saint martyred. The frivolous one triumphs, the cheater wins the game, arrogant and tyrannical officials determine the fates of a people. A group and a Christian community may be led by mediocre sycophants of the powerful. In such a setting praying "may your will be done" requires being committed to justice, to a relationship that includes everyone, and to a strong sense of the common good. And simultaneously, aware of our insufficiencies, we abandon ourselves to the Mystery of God, who knows when to step in and guarantee a happy end to the drama of history. Doing God's will "on earth as it is in heaven" means doing God's will not occasionally, but always, in each and every circumstance, everywhere and at all times. Otherwise, we are not strengthening the reign, which seeks to advance into history.

"*Our daily bread.*" This is the second part of Jesus' message. If we stop to think about it, it is in line with the two basic impulses of the human heart: one toward the Father, his reign, and his will; and the other toward the necessary bread without which we cannot live, forgiveness, and the overcoming of all the evil that continually stigmatizes us.

Bread represents human food. It reveals to us our essential connectedness to the material infrastructure of life. No matter how high the flights of the spirit, no matter how deep the mystical plunge into the divine essence, we all depend on a little bread and water to assure our life. A dead person has no experience of mysticism and does not praise God. Life is more than bread, but it cannot do without it at any time. Materiality has a sacramental character, for it is bound to life. The eternal future of life is decided in the infrastructure: whether we have given bread to the hungry, water to the thirsty, clothing to the naked. The destiny of all, blessed and accursed, is at stake in this minimum solidarity (Mt 25:31–40).

In establishing the counterpoint between our Father and our daily bread, Jesus wanted there to be not only God's cause—the reign—but the cause of human beings—bread—with their needs, their hunger, their urgencies. Human beings are there not just for God. They are also there for themselves and for one another. That is what God wanted. He didn't want us only to love him; he wanted our love to go out in all directions. We should love his creation, all beings, and each actual person. We will be in the inheritance of Jesus only if we always associate our Father with our bread, God's cause with the human cause, and the cause of the heavens with the cause of the earth.

The need for bread is individual; it cannot be satisfied, however, individually, but only in community. Hence, Jesus does not command us to pray *my* bread, but *our* bread. That is so because with Jesus the full awareness of universal kinship resulting from universal sonhood and daughterhood broke forth. We have an *Abba*-Father who is of all—our Father—and so we are all sons and daughters, in the Son, brothers and sisters among ourselves. Mere individual satisfaction of hunger without taking into consideration the hunger of our other brothers and sisters would be a violation of the kinship willed by Jesus. Human beings want more than simply satisfying hunger and being nourished. Eating is always being at the table with others, a community act, and rite of communion. That is why we break bread at the table. One who satisfies his hunger alone does not eat happily, knowing that the Lazaruses are at the foot of the table, with the dogs, waiting for the remains of our abundance. Bread is only human, our bread as in Jesus' prayer, when it is produced together, broken together, and made bond of communion among all.

To the bread is added the expression *of each day*. What is of each day is what is necessary. From Jesus' eschatological standpoint, the Greek expression *epioúsios* (daily, of each day) may also be given another translation, along the lines of the apocalyptic mentality of Jesus: give us now today tomorrow's bread, that of the great advent of the reign. The various possible interpretations matter little. The Our Father as prayed in the post-Jesus communities, no longer apocalyptic and within ongoing history, simply means the bread we need day by day in order to live and survive.

What matters is holding on to the unity between our Father and our bread. There are those who concentrate on the "our Father"; they sing, dance, and rejoice in having a Father in heaven who is preparing a reign for us, forgetting the "our bread," and with it the yelping of the hungry that rises from earth to heaven. There are others who generously strive to create conditions so that all will have sufficient daily bread, resulting from a social change in which all work together to make the bread "our bread," and forget the "our Father"; in doing so they are not concerned with satisfying the insatiable hunger for an infinite warm embrace that cannot be given by bread but only by God. Both separate what Jesus brought together. We are not allowed to break this sacred alliance. Only by uniting our Father with our bread can we sincerely say: Amen. We cannot lose the essential unified perspective of Jesus' message: uniting reign with history, our Father with our bread, the divine cause with the human cause. Only thus is salvation comprehensive and does history find its true direction.

"Forgive us our debts." There is an undeniable cosmic fact: we are all interdependent; we need one another to live and survive. That is the source of the positive feelings of gratitude, reciprocity, and debt. Beyond personal effort we owe almost all we are and do to those who are our neighbors, but above all to divine grace, which permeates all things. We are indeed debtors. This debt does not humiliate us; it merely shows our human poverty and our need for one another. This is an innocent and natural relationship, but we can do something that only we as persons can do: not maintain this mutuality, this giving-receiving-and-returning. We can break this logic of gift and take the other's necessary bread, in other words, snatch the little he or she has to pay a debt that we have incurred for any reason.

That is what is done by the major world economic lending agencies that collect debt with abusive interest. Peoples are sacrificed to serve the banks that mercilessly collect the debts, even when children are dying of hunger and disease and a whole society enters into a serious crisis of sustainability. Jesus was aware of the harshness of the policy of collecting the many debts made up of the taxes collected for the empire, for the temple, to maintain the priestly caste, to sustain the state apparatus, and for public security. The people were crying out under the weight of debt, especially in Galilee, which produced a lot of food and had many debtors, fearful that the little they had would be taken from them. In the new order established in the reign, rather than debt it will be the solidarity economy of gift and debt forgiveness that will prevail. It was in the proposal of Jesus, when he launched his program in the synagogue of Nazareth (Lk 4:18–21), which entailed the liberation of the oppressed to also announce "a year of grace of the Lord" (v. 19). This year of grace of the Lord was understood as an eschatological sign, that is, a sign of the ultimate coming of the reign, when all debts would be forgiven. All things would be reconciled. The wounds that we have inflicted on creation would be completely healed.

However, there is an aspect of debt that is not material but moral and spiritual, that which we feel before God, who is revealed as so good. We are sinners. Our conscience won't stop blaming us and making us responsible. We have here a debt of conscience. How do we refashion the bond of communion with God and with the other? Jesus invents a formula for paying this debt and is clear about it: "Forgive and you shall be forgiven" (Lk 6:37). We sin every day, and often. We feel that we are vulnerable and that alone we are unable to realize our dreams and our ideals. We are left with an unpayable debt, and it is then that we hear the consoling word of divine remission: "If our heart accuses us, greater than our heart is God" (1 Jn 3:20). It is part of Jesus' message to present *Abba*-God as the Father of infinite mercy, who is remission of all debt. He asks us, "Be merciful as your Father is merciful" (Lk 6:36). Those who experience the unrestricted full mercy of the Father must live it toward those who have offended them and have acquired a moral debt toward God. That is how the "as we forgive" should be understood. It is not a negotiation with God or the establishment of a prior condition; rather, it is about maintaining the same attitude toward others that the Father has toward us. If we receive full forgiveness from God, complete remission of our debt to him, we must also give full forgiveness and complete remission to anyone who has offended us. It is a single movement, that of merciful love. How can someone who is unwilling to forgive his or her brothers and sisters receive God's forgiveness? The reign of God entails such mutuality.

"And do not let us fall into temptation." This is a plea that translates the bitter existential experience that we are weak beings, subject to the temptation to betray the hopes and promises of the reign. We fail to make sustainable the goods of the reign that we take on with solidarity and unconditional love for all. We fall into the old pattern of the world, cantered on self-affirmation and arrogance. We have to struggle against ourselves, deal with renunciation, for the forces of pleasure, personal advantage, and social status attract us and promise us a fulfillment that we later discover to be illusory. It is the daily temptation fed by the consumption propaganda machine. If we fall into it, that portion of the reign that has been won is lost. The reign does not advance. We feel chained to forces that hold us hostage. The only real disaster of the human being is to have fallen historically into temptation and to keep doing so. The great refusal is ever renewed. Saint James noted rightly: "God . . . tempts no one. But one is tempted by one's own desire, being lured and enticed by it" (Jas 1:13–14). Such is the human condition, and not even Jesus was exempted from it; he was "surrounded by weakness" (Heb 5:2) and "was tempted and so he can help those who are tempted" (Heb 5:7). He felt the power of temptation, but he resisted for he "offered up prayers and supplications, with loud cries and tears" (Heb 5:7). Trembling he prays, "Father, let this cup pass from me" (Mt 26:39). Temptation accompanied Jesus his whole life, to the point where he praised the disciples for having stood by him "in my temptations" (Lk 22:28). But the moment of the great temptation is coming, the final confrontation between the reign and the empire, between Christ and the great seducer, between the Son of God and the son of perdition (2 Thes 2:3), as is stated in scripture: "iniquity will overflow and charity will grow cold in many" (Mt 24:12). The great "adversary who raises himself against everything that is divine and sacred and presents himself as though he were God" (2 Thes 2:4), man of iniquity, will use the symbols of Christ, and perform miracles, and many will follow him. It is at this final moment that the agonizing cry arises from those who have chosen the reign: "Do not let us fall into temptation," into defection and apostasy. And then they

will hear the words of promise: "Take courage, I have overcome the world" (Jn 16:33).

"Deliver us from evil." Evil exists and is the powerful force of the negative in history. It has its perverse logic and its seductions, because it never presents itself as evil. Evil is not so much a perverse person hostile to life, but rather a set of malign forces and movement of ideas, a historic drive, spread throughout all realms of human activity, which places the individual good above the collective good, practices deceit, and spreads lies to obtain advantages, "imprisoning truth in injustice" (Rom 1:18). It is capable of torture and myriad cruelties, including murder. It can even jeopardize the very existence of the human species and destroy the ecological conditions of life on the planet, as the prophet Isaiah foresaw (24:3–6). This current is embodied in systems of values that are actually anti-values, in leaders who coordinate and promote strategies of evil. It is not felt as evil but as a fortunate and proper response to the circumstances, what is best for humankind, when it is only best for them. Evil becomes a cultural, economic, and political system, conquers even religions, and is internalized in people's lives and keeps them hostage in their anti-values and evil habits. When evil is no longer perceived as evil, but rather is lived out as normal and natural, it reaches its climax. In his sense of the world as apocalyptic, Jesus grasped this long before Nietzsche, this inversion of values and the temptation that it can signify. We can embrace evil intending to do good. The petition in the Our Father, "Deliver us from evil," assumes that humankind is inexorably on its way toward the end point when everything is at stake. On this ultimate journey all obstacles appear, all chasms open wide, and the danger of defection is imminent. The empire attacks with all its weapons to get at the heart of the reign. The original meaning of "deliver us from evil" is not that the evil be removed, for it is in history, but that in our life journey God give us the strength to confront it and to be stronger and more steadfast than it, that he free us from the imminence of falling into the abyss and betraying the dream of the reign. It is in this context that the believer cries out: "Father, deliver us from evil, protect us from apostasy and do

not abandon us at this moment." It is a boundless consolation to hear from Jesus: "If you ask anything in my name, I will do it" (Jn 14:14); "Take courage, raise your heads because your liberation is coming near" (Lk 21:28); "I have overcome the world" (Jn 15:18).

The energy of the Amen. The Our Father as Jesus' personal message encompasses the entire human trajectory in its impulse toward heaven (our Father) and in its rootedness in the earth (our bread). Jesus grasps the sym-bolic and dia-bolic aspect. He does not deny any dimension of the human drama but infuses the hope that humanity and the entire creation will end well. That is why he ends with the Amen. The Amen is the radical YES to reality, despite the chaos and the tribulation of desolation. They will not triumph. "The Lord Jesus will destroy the evil one with the breath of his mouth" (2 Thes 2:8). This is the great promise that remains to be fulfilled, that will be fulfilled in the time determined by the Mystery.

The parables: Metaphors of the reign. The beatitudes are another indication of Jesus' underlying intention. We are going to take them up below when dealing with Jesus' ethic, but besides the Our Father and the parables, his forty-one parables are also indications of Jesus' primary intention *(ipsissima intentio Jesu)*. Even though they have been reworked theologically and literarily by the authors of the four Gospels, their core is from Jesus and display an originality and freshness that we rarely find in the First Testament. They appear as strong metaphors of the presence and action of the reign of God. They are snapshots of that time, charged with vitality and proximity to everyday life. They are aimed at clarifying the nature of the already present reign, in process, and yet to come. Some are unforgettable, like that of the prodigal son (Lk 15:11–32), the good Samaritan (Lk 10:25–37), the rich glutton and the poor man Lazarus (Lk 16:1–7), the arrogant Pharisee and the humble tax collector (Lk 18:9–14), the wheat and the chaff (Mt 13:24–30, 36–43), the great supper (Lk 14:16–24), and the scene of the final judgment (Mt 25:31–46).

To conclude. With Jesus there has begun an accelerated process of the approach and fulfillment of the reign as total revolution and liberation of the universe, of humankind, and of people's lives, but this reign is not assured. It depends on the adherence of people who are widening the space where the reign is embodied in love, forgiveness, compassion, thirst for justice, fidelity to the truth, total confidence, and surrender to *Abba*-God, and in acceptance of his Son. This reign lives under the temptation of being frustrated, denied, and ultimately rejected. Dramatically, that is what happened. The prophet who proclaimed it, Jesus, was eliminated. However, the dream did not die with him. Is there any sign, however, that he will one day be able to triumph truly and completely? Otherwise, the dream that remains dream amounts to a fantasy and flight from reality. Was Jesus deceived, a dreamer? We wonder anxiously. But there are signs that sustain us and keep us hoping and accepting his proposal.

5. An ethic: Unlimited love and mercy

It isn't preaching that saves but practices. This is the basic key to the ethic of Jesus. Which practices align people with the great dream of the reign of God, those that save? These practices do not sacralize, or extend, or improve existing ones. They start new ones. For new wine, new wineskins; for new music, new ears.

The first thing Jesus does in terms of ethics and behavior is free the human being. We all live behind the bars of laws, rules, prescriptions, traditions, rewards, and punishments. That is how religions and societies work; with such instruments they make people fit in, keep them submissive, create the established order. Jesus stands up to this kind of apparatus, which impedes the exercise of freedom and stifles energy: "You have heard that it was said to the ancients, but I say to you" (Mt 5:21–22). Since he is apocalyptic, he lives an ethic of urgency. Clock time is running against history. There is no halfway point: "Let your word be yes if it is yes and no if it is no" (Mt 5:37). What is most important about the law is not observing the traditions and fulfilling religious precepts, but "doing justice, mercy, and good faith" (Mt 23:23).

The essential and new thing introduced by Jesus is unconditional love. Love of neighbor and love of God are the same thing, and the meaning of all the biblical tradition is to culminate in this unity (Mt 22:37:40). The radical proposal resounds: "Love as I have loved you," which is love to the end (Jn 13:34). No one is excluded from love, not even enemies, for God loves all, even the "ungrateful and wicked" (Lk 6:35).

The law of Christ—if indeed this word *law* can be used—or rather the logic of the reign, is encapsulated in love. This love is more than a feeling and a passion. It is a decision for freedom; it is a life purpose in the sense of always opening oneself to others, letting them be, listening to them, welcoming them, and if they fall, reaching out to them. The truth of this love is tested in whether we love the vulnerable, the despised, and the invisible. It is especially of our relationship of acceptance of these wretched of the earth that Jesus is thinking when he asks us to love one another or the neighbor. Making this love the standard of moral behavior entails demanding of the human being something highly difficult and uncomfortable. It is easier to live within laws and prescriptions that anticipate and determine everything. One lives boxed in but at ease. Jesus came to tear down this inertia and to awaken human beings from this ethical slumber. He invites them, for the sake of love, to create conduct appropriate to each moment; he urges them to be alert and creative. The reign is set up whenever this loving and absolutely open and accepting stance exists. If power means anything, it is to be a potency of service. Power is only ethical if it enhances the power of the other and fosters relationships of love and cooperation among all; otherwise, the domination of some over others continues, and we become entangled in the nets of the interests in contention.

This love is expressed radically in the Sermon on the Mount. There Jesus makes a clear option for victims and for those who don't count in the present order. He declares that the blessed, that is, bearers of the divine blessings, are the poor, and that the first heirs of the reign are those who weep, the meek, those who hunger and thirst for justice, the compassionate, the pure of heart, the peacemakers, those who are persecuted for the sake of justice, those who bear insults and persecutions for the sake of the reign and put up with lies and every kind of evil (Mt 5:3–12). Indeed, the ethic of Jesus reaches even into people's innermost and hidden intentions: not only those who kill but even those who offend their brothers and sisters will be liable (Mt 5:22); even desiring another's wife suffices for committing adultery in one's heart (Mt 5:28). He states emphatically: "Do not resist the evil; if someone slaps your right cheek, offer him your left; if someone disputes with you to take your clothing, offer him your cloak as well" (Mt 5:39–40). It was such ideals of Jesus that led Thoreau, Tolstoy, Gandhi, and Dom Hélder Câmara to propose the way of active nonviolence for confronting the power of the negative.

How is this radicalism to be understood? What matters is knowing that Jesus did not come to bring a harsher law or an improved phariseeism. We will completely lose the perspective of the historic Jesus if we interpret the Sermon on the Mount and his moral indications within the framework of the law. He renders its fulfillment impossible. Or else, human beings are left in despair, as seems to have happened with Luther. What is new with Jesus is that he brings good news: it isn't the law that saves, but love, which knows no limits. There are limits to law, because its function is to create order and guarantee some harmony among people in society and to curb those who violate it. Jesus did not come simply to abolish "the law and the prophets" (Mt 5:17). He came to lay out a criterion: what comes from traditions and moral rules, if it passes through the sieve of love, will be accepted. If laws impede and hinder love, he relativizes them, as he did with the Sabbath, or he ignores them, as he did with the precept of fasting. It is love that opens up the reign. Where power prevails, the doors and windows of love, communication, solidarity, and mercy close. That applies to both society and the churches.

The supreme ideal of the ethic of Jesus is proclaimed in "Be perfect as the Father is perfect" (5:48). Jesus always emphasizes two characteristics of the Father's perfection: a love for all without barriers and an unlimited mercy. Love and mercy guide those who wish to enter the reign. It is not enough to be good and law abiding, like the brother of the prodigal son who stayed home and was faithful in all things. That is not enough. We have to be loving and merciful. Unless these attitudes are internalized, the reign does not advance, even though it is already set in motion by the practice of Jesus. When the reign is established, we will witness the great revolution in the sense of the spirit of the beatitudes: the poor will feel like citizens of the reign, those who weep will feel consoled, the nonviolent will possess and administer the earth, those who hunger and thirst for justice will see their dreams fulfilled, those who have compassion for others will experience mercy, the pure of heart will experience God directly, the peacemakers will be recognized as sons and daughters of God, those persecuted for the sake of justice will feel that they are heirs of the reign, and those who were insulted and persecuted for the sake of the dream of Jesus will be especially blessed (cf. Mt 5:3–11). Never have values been so radically reversed, as here courageously proposed by Jesus.

What is the ultimate meaning of the Sermon on the Mount, the contents of which we have just set forth and which sum up the fundamental ethic of the Jesus of history? It isn't a new law or a new ethical and moral ideal. It is something quite different. It is about establishing a criterion for measuring how far along we are on the path of the reign, near the reign or within the reign, or how far away we are, out of alignment and outside it. The Sermon on the Mount is an invitation and a challenge to us to do our utmost at this last hour, to approach the ideals that make up the content of the reign. The reign is about to break in. The colliding meteor is about to enter the earth's atmosphere and set the earth on fire. The shortest and surest route to entering the reign of God is to participate in this way in the dream of Jesus and to live unconditional love and unlimited mercy now. That is the infallible passport for entering the reign and participating in the life of the Trinity. There is no reason to fear the devastation wrought by the colliding meteor because it leads to the emergence of a new world and a transfigured humanity.

6.   A destiny: The execution of the liberator

Jesus didn't die in a sickbed or of old age. He was executed on the cross. His court-ordered assassination is the result of his life, his preaching, his liberating practice, the consciousness that he had developed of his connection to the *Abba*-Father, and his connection to the reign, something that very much scandalized the religious authorities and placed him under suspicion as a subversive by the representatives of the Roman Empire.

From the outset (Mk 3:6) his life was enveloped in conflicts prompted by the freedom he took toward the oppressions that religion and traditions imposed on believers. Jesus travels a path of courage. He takes sides whenever it is a matter of defending the right and dignity of the other, whether that person is a heretic, pagan, foreigner, riffraff, prostitute, public sinner, child, sick person, or other on the margins. He unmasked the falsity of legalistic religion. He had to confront two trials: one religious and the other political.

In the *religious* realm they made all kinds of accusations against him. Three stand out: The first is connected to freedom toward the Torah, the Sabbath, and the purification laws, which leads to scandalizing and subverting the people. The second is the *strict connection* that Jesus establishes between himself and the reign he proclaims. Accepting the reign entails accepting its proclaimer, Jesus, for message and messenger are the same. That was scandalous; on what grounds does someone weak and unknown, with insufficient means for such a high mission, claim to be initiating the reign, which was believed to be of glory and victory? The third and decisive reason is that of allowing a glimpse at a most special *relationship with God.* He calls God *Abba*-Father and presents himself simply as Son, in absolute terms. This involves nothing less than invading the divine space. It is blasphemy. It was the evangelist John who best expressed the reason for the condemnation of Jesus: "he called God his own Father, making himself equal to God" (Jn 5:16). In its strict monotheism, Judaism was not in a position to hear and accept a word like this, born of a new consciousness. It would amount to betraying the essence of Jewish faith.

In the *political* realm the main reason for his condemnation was the fact that Jesus proclaimed the reign of God, which stands directly opposed to the empire of Caesar. The claim of the Caesars was that they were to be regarded and adored as gods, and some even called themselves *deus de deo*, a title that Christens would later apply to Jesus in the Creed. To the ears of the Roman Empire, proclaiming the reign of God meant proposing an alternative to the empire of Caesar. That was tantamount to political subversion (Lk 23:2, 14). Interrogated directly by the Roman authority whether he was king, Jesus first with utter assurance gave an evasive reply, not assuming that he was king. Afterward, he explicitly reaffirmed it, but the king and reign in question are of another nature. This accusation that he was the proclaimer of a reign sufficed for him to be condemned in the typical manner of the period: crucifixion. The order was given, correctly, that "Jesus of Nazareth, King of the Jews" be written at the top of the cross in three languages, Latin, Greek, and Hebrew. For the Romans he was a mock king, and the crown could only be one of thorns.

Did Jesus expect violent death? What can be drawn from the texts closest to his apocalyptic mindset was that he felt so close to *Abba*-God that God would save him at the last moment. In apocalyptic circles they spoke of the "great temptation" through which the Messiah would pass. The technical terms used were "the hour" and "drinking the chalice." Traces of this mindset of Jesus are found in the account of the temptation of Gethsemane. Jesus fears that decisive moment when the proclaimer of the reign and the great adversary, representing the empire, would confront one another decisively. Jesus prays: "My soul is sad even unto death" (Mk 14:34). He pleads: "Father, let this hour pass from me" (Mk 14:35). Amid supplications and tears he appeals: "*Abba*, Father, everything is possible for you; remove this chalice [this is the apocalyptic word] from me, but let not what I want but what you want be done" (Mk 14:36). In one of its critical versions the epistle to the Hebrews comments that God did not hear his prayers: "Although he was

Son of God, he learned obedience through what he suffered" (Heb 5:7–8). What matters is holding on to this fundamental stance of Jesus: being faithful to *Abba*-Father, and understanding himself on that basis rather than from himself. God would save him, but at the supreme moment, as he is about to die, he realizes that God will not step in or save him. He abandons him and simply turns him over to death. Jesus feels the hell of this abandonment by God. He expires with an anguished cry flung out to the infinite (Mk 14:37). It is the ultimate stripping, it is the complete surrender of his own will. He surrenders to the design of Mystery, regardless of what it is. Personal resurrection is God's response to this stripping and radical faithfulness to God: a life that is no longer under the empire of death and that ushers in the new. Only one who is completely empty can be utterly fulfilled.

With the death sentence announced, the torture procedures follow; they were barbaric and even included sexual abuse. Jesus suffers everything with deep resignation, like a sheep aware that he is going to slaughter. He carries the cross, the instrument of death, on his own shoulders, aided by the peasant Simon of Cyrene. He is nailed to it and lifted up between two thieves. Besides spiritual and psychological sufferings, Jesus undergoes a terrifying spiritual suffering: feeling the "death" of God. Any expectation of the intervention of the *Abba*-God in keeping with his apocalyptic belief suddenly disappears. The cry he utters before dying (Mk 14:37) reveals the limits of disillusionment. Then he expires. What continuity will there be? Has the dream died? Has it evaporated with its bearer?

7. An anticipation: The resurrection scarcely begun

The prophet has failed. He has left the world protesting and uttering a great cry of frustration (Mk 15:34). He no longer cries out for *Abba*-Father. He simply cries for him as God: *"Eloi, Eloi lemá sabachtahni!"* (My God, my God, why have you abandoned me?)

(Mk 15:34). The nameless God-Mystery, boundless Mystery, has shown its character of Mystery to itself and to Jesus.

But Jesus held on to the dream to the end, to the edge of despair. We do not know what happened in Jesus' inner depth. We know that he continued to cry for "*My* God," which implies a final and despairing reference to him whom he would never abandon and to whom he would always be faithful. He never betrayed God or himself or his line of action. He remained faithful to God, even within the existential hell of brutal death. God seemingly may have abandoned Jesus. Jesus did not abandon God. To the very end he showed what he always was: the Son, someone radically for others, he who completely strips himself, to the point of assuring the victory of the reign. Finally, he surrenders, defeated, this suffering servant and persecuted prophet, to the Unnameable, whose design seems truly mysterious to him. Will he again refer to *Abba*-Father? St. Luke may have translated without error the final stance of the failed Prophet: "*Abba*, into your hands I surrender my spirit" (Lk 23:46). He has felt once more that he is Son and so continues calling God *Abba*-Father.

And the reign? It barely got started. Very few joined in. It became an open reality, handed over to the will of those who insist and do not desist, those who believe that the utopian is truer than the factual, and that the last word that the universe is going to hear and re-echo from point to point of its space will be "all is consummated" (Jn 19:30); that is, all will reach its culmination, everything will finish being born; Trinity-God will finally say: "all is good." He utters that word only at the end of history, not at its beginning, because not everything "is good" within it, as can be shown at any time. When will "all is good" be heard? The Genesis text, "all is good," is prophetic and points to an open future. But when will this moment of the in-breaking after the failure of Jesus be? There remained a glimmer of hope in the form of future prophecy preserved in Revelation, the Book of Consolation: "I saw a new heaven and a new earth. . . . God will dwell among men definitively. All peoples will be people of God. He will wipe away the tears from their eyes, and death will no longer exist, nor will be there mourning, or weeping, or fatigue, because all this has passed away" (Rv 21:1, 4). Really? Is it an imaginary dream or the promise of a real future?

If this dream has no anticipatory sign, it will remain a dream, and it will be hard to distinguish it from the projection of desire that does not find routes to realization anywhere. Sheer dream, torn away from history, is tantamount to alienation and to flight from the brutality of facts. It would mean simply the confirmation of the absurdity of the human condition and of the fate of the universe.

But, surprisingly, an anticipatory sign has occurred, grasped by a woman, a close friend, Mary of Magdala (Jn 20:11–18). She tells the apostles: "Jesus lives." That proclamation caused more fear than joy, but the proclamation slowly took hold. It was first interpreted within the apocalyptic categories that were familiar to Jesus, as "elevation and justification of the suffering servant." God had not abandoned his servant, as it seemed. Now he has restored him, bringing him to life. At this point the talk was still not of resurrection. Only later, for apologetic reasons facing Christians from Hellenistic culture, did talk of resurrection begin. In the Greek view the return to the body is no benefit; it is rather a punishment, since the body represents the prison *(sema)* of the soul in the body *(soma)*, the death of which would mean its liberation. Returning to the body by resurrection is going back and reentering prison. To avoid this type of cultural understanding, Christians began to use the expression *resurrection* in a new sense, not simply as the reanimation of a corpse, as with Lazarus, but as a new type of body—"spiritual body" (1 Cor 15:44), a real body, but one that takes on the dimensions of the spirit, and so transfigured, free of the imprisonment of space and time, a cosmic body. Thus it emerges as "the brand new Adam," expression of the new creation, as Saint Paul says (cf. 1 Cor 15:45).

But the decisive fact and the high point of the evolutionary process thus far has happened; a tiny sign that the dream is not a total failure has been announced. There is something of the resurrection, a small anticipation, in the world. It was Origen, perhaps Christianity's greatest theological genius, who expressed precisely the meaning of this anticipation: the resurrection is the *autobasileia tou Theou*—the realization of the reign of God only in the person of Jesus. The reign cannot be fulfilled universally due to collective human rejection, but it is fulfilled incipiently in the person of Jesus. It is an incipient fulfillment, that is, scarcely the beginning of the reign. People have not been conquered by the reign, societies have not been organized around the goods of the reign, the universe has only been slightly touched by this initial inauguration, but there is something there, in seed form, with all the power of the seed, to show the happy end of the universe in miniature. Jesus himself has not finished rising. He has begun in himself the process of resurrection, in other words, of the embodiment of what the reign of God means. Only his personal core has risen. Only him. As long as his brothers and sisters, as long as the *Lebenswelt* has not been enlivened, and as long the universe has not been transfigured, his resurrection has not reached complete fulfillment. It represents an open dynamism. Jesus continues to be resurrected in the world, although now by sharing in the life of the crucified, his brothers and sisters, until, in the fullness of time, he finishes being resurrected. He still has future. The resurrection is still under way. It is shown in the goods of the reign and resurrection, such as in love, solidarity, dignity, the defense of the weak, and care for our common home, the earth.

The appearances narrated in the Gospels were elaborated subsequently for apologetic purposes, and their value as history is not very reliable. The Gospel of Mark, the oldest of all, written in the 60s, after the execution of Jesus on the cross, offers, in our view, the true interpretation along the lines that we are presenting here. It is unaware of visions and appearances of the Risen One; it simply acknowledges that Jesus arose (16:6). That is how his Gospel ends, at chapter 16, verse 8. The stories of appearances that it narrates are viewed by critical scholarship as a subsequent addition, made in the second century, summarizing what is in the other Gospels. In any case, the living Jesus, through the women, tells the apostles that they will be able to see him in Galilee (Mk 16:7). Matthew still retains this old memory, having the angel say to the women: "Then go quickly and tell his disciples, 'He has been raised from the dead, and indeed he is going ahead of you to Galilee; there you will see him'" (Mt 28:7). This means particularly that we are still being invited to go to Galilee in order to see the Risen One there. We have been on the road to Galilee for over two thousand years, with the expectation that the Risen One will come and be made manifest in his fullness. He has still not been made manifest, thereby justifying the testimony of the evangelist Matthew who says, after all the claimed appearances, "Some of the disciples are still doubting" (Mt 28:17). We are still on the road, some doubting; others, like us, trusting and driven by the hope that does not want to die, are heading toward Galilee.

The world still goes on its way. The horrors marking human history do not diminish. Where have we improved? We do not seem to have improved, and the resurrection seems not to have occurred. In fact, Jesus has still not shown all his transforming power present in his risen core, nor has he confirmed the final victory of the reign. So, unfortunately, the always ambiguous logic of things, sym-bolic and dia-bolic, continues as though there had been no redemption, and that no anticipatory sign of resurrection had been given. Indeed, all is so inchoate, initial, potential, and seminal that it does not leave uncontestable traces in history. This invalidates all discourses of the exalting of Jesus, of the self-glorification of the churches and triumphalism, found especially in religious hymns, as though a rescue of creation, societies, and persons had already fully taken place. It has barely begun to happen. Such discourse makes sense only within a perspective of hope and prophecy, something that is still going to occur in the future, but actually no transformation that is visible and perceptible to the senses has happened: corruption persists, the churches are still closer to the palaces than to the manger, and people still need to struggle hard against the demons dwelling in them so that their better angels can survive, even though they can counsel us and arouse hope in the realization of the dream of Jesus.

The reign barely moves forward; the goods of the reign achieve some visibility against the ravages of the empire of wickedness when the sacredness of life is safeguarded, creation is respected, the vulnerable are defended, bread is distributed to the hungry, pardon is offered to the evil, and the seductions of this evil world, which persists in denying, distorting, lying, oppressing, torturing, and murdering innocent lives and entire ethnic groups and ecosystems, are resisted. The plea "thy kingdom come" is always in order. How long Lord? Until when must we wait? When will we finally come to Galilee to contemplate full resurrection? Nowhere are we given an answer. We have to believe and hope. Paul pragmatically says, "Only in hope will we be saved" (Rom 8:24). And for hope, a philosopher has said, "Genesis is at the end, not at the beginning." And how we yearn for it to be made manifest!

4.

Christianity and History

Jesus left an *opus inconclusum*, an unfinished work. Since the reign did not come in its desired plenitude, only in his person through the resurrection, in its stead have come the Jesus movement, the churches, folk Christianity, and the Christian values that have made their way into Western and indeed world culture. This new phase cannot be regarded as the deterioration of the previous one; it is simply something else. There now begins the history of the influence of the dream of Jesus and its preservation through the writings that gathered his words and deeds—the four Gospels and the other texts of the Second Testament—and primarily the Christian churches. It slowly begins to spread into the world outside and to take root in continents and cultures. This process shares in the condition of real history, ever marked by moments of violence and of peace, of mendacious pacts and heroic deeds. The dia-bolic and sym-bolic dimensions have not spared Christianity. Sometimes the dia-bolic takes on calamitous proportions that have nothing to do with the legacy of Jesus; at other times the sym-bolic has reached the pinnacles of perfection and has shown the possibility of the anticipation, albeit partial, of the reign of God. There are the saints, the martyrs, the mystics, and the piety of so many simple people who have taken seriously the cause of Jesus.

1. The distinction between reign of God and the church

The foregoing leads us, first of all to distinguish between reign of God and church. They are neither overlapping nor identified. The phenomenon and word *church* do not even exist for the evangelists Mark, Luke, and John. Rightly so, because it wasn't in Jesus' plans. Everything was concentrated on the reign. It was only late, around 90 CE, when the tragic end of Jesus had been assimilated and Christian communities had been set up, that the Gospel of Matthew emerges with this word *church*. He connects it to Jesus and to Peter's faith. Until the fifth century, the text of Matthew 16:17–19, "You are Peter and upon this rock I will build my church," was understood by both the Catholic and Orthodox churches as praise by Jesus for Peter's faith, and it was not taken to point to the foundation of the church. The church will be built on *this faith*, not on the *person* of Peter. That finding is important for relativizing the subsequent interpretation by those governing the Roman Catholic Church, which sought and still seeks its self-justification as the only true church in succession from the apostle Peter. Peter's merit was that of professing faith in Jesus as Son of God (Mt 16:18; 18:17) before the other apostles. It is on *this faith*, therefore, and not on the *figure of Peter*, subsequently disqualified by Jesus as satan, that the Christian community is to be built, constituted by those who believe as Peter believed. Indeed, in wrongly understanding the concept of Son of God, which was not that of power and glory but of renunciation and humiliation, Peter, as we have already noted, is roughly rebuked, with the harshest expression that Jesus used, calling him "satan" and "stumbling block" (Mt 16:23).

The church only comes into play because the reign could not be definitively established and because there was a basis for sustaining it: Peter's faith. The reign is the key thing; the church is secondary. The reign is the whole; the church, the part. The reign is the substance; the church its sign-sacrament. The reign will remain; the church will disappear. Hence, it will never be possible to identify reign with church. At most it may be said that the church is the sacrament, sign, and instrument of the reign, just as it can unfortunately be said to be the anti-sacrament of the reign. Its greatest merit is that of preserving the sacred memory of Jesus, not letting his dream die, creating conditions for anticipating it in history with initiatives arising out of love and compassion, but it can also be a hindrance to the gospel by the way it is organized: hierarchical, authoritarian, and doctrinaire. The reality of the institutional church is paradoxical, both holy and sinner, or as it came to be said in the early centuries, *casta meretrix*, a chaste harlot, chaste when it is in line with the gospel, harlot when it betrays it.

2. Christianity as movement and spiritual way

Christianity first appeared in history as a *way (odós tou Christou)* and as a *movement,* that is, prior to its sedimentation in the Gospels, doctrines, rituals, and churches. The character of spiritual way and movement is something perennial and has ever been maintained throughout history; it is a type of Christianity that has its own route. It generally lives on the margin and sometimes at a critical distance from the official institution, but it arises out of and is nourished from the ongoing fascination for the figure of Jesus of Nazareth and for his liberating and spiritual message. Initially regarded as heresy of the Nazarenes (Acts 24:5), or simply "heresy" (Acts 28:22) in the sense of "little group," it slowly gained autonomy until its followers were called Christians, as attested in the Acts of the Apostles (11:36). The Jesus movement is certainly the greatest strength of Christianity because it is not boxed in to institutions or imprisoned in doctrines and dogmas. It is made up of all kinds of people, from the most varied cultures and spiritual traditions, even agnostics and atheists who let themselves be deeply touched by his courageous figure, his freedom-loving spirit, his deeply humanistic message, his ethic of unconditional love, especially for the poor and oppressed, and by the way he took on the drama of human destiny, in the midst of humiliation, torture, and execution on the cross. He presented an image of God that was so close and friendly to life that it is hard to get away from it, even for someone who doesn't believe in God. Many say: If there is a God, it must be the one that has the features of the God of Jesus. They all feel attracted and close to his ideals and manner of life. The Jesus movement stands out as a high form of humanism and reveals a religious belief, but also a nonreligious belief in the value of the human person, including his or her transcendent dimension.

3.   Christianity encountering cultures

From being a movement Christianity very early took on the shape of family groups, small Christian communities and institutional churches with various forms of organization. Within them the many Christologies exalting his figure were developed. Out of them emerged the Gospels, which collected the contents of faith of the respective communities. These are two-sided: *power* and *charism*. Sacred power serves for the organizing internal order and establishing the criteria of belonging and exclusion; a set of doctrines is defined as an identifying reference point, ethical norms are established to be followed by everyone, and its own styles of celebration are created. This is the Petrine dimension of the church, that is, maintaining what Peter signifies: tradition and the fact that his faith constitutes the perennial foundation of the Christian phenomenon. Through charism tradition is loosened, new visions are projected, other languages are created, prophetic figures are supported, and innovations emerging from dialogue with the surroundings are accepted. That is the Pauline dimension of the church, that is, recognizing what was done by Paul, who without asking anyone, began his evangelization within the Greek world, reinventing Christianity in the garb of that culture, and having the courage to innovate in order to respond to different situations. The church is charism and power; both elements coexist and have equal dignity. Unfortunately, power has marginalized, if not stifled, charism, without ever entirely succeeding, rigidifying the message of Jesus to the point where it loses its liberating character and its lure. However, it is from the pole of charism that the pole of power in the church-institution should be understood; otherwise it sets itself apart and takes away the vitality and radiance of the dream of Jesus.

Thus, from the outset, the communities developed different faces: some of a Judaic style, others marked by diaspora Judaism, yet others by the dominant Roman culture, and finally, ones characterized by the Hellenism that was spread throughout the empire. Later, the church took on the form of Germanic, Hispanic, and general European culture. In colonized countries on the margins of the great course of history and of the church, it took on, through incarnation into local cultures, African and Asian traces, and in the Americas, Indian-Afro-Latin American features. More than half of all Christians live in these churches, and so today we can say that Christianity is a religion of the Third and Fourth Worlds and no longer of the central Northern Hemisphere countries. In Ethiopia and North Africa it took on African features, and in Asia Minor, Middle Eastern styles. Insofar as the dream of Jesus takes flesh in these different situations, it limits itself, but at the same time it opens the way to new expressions, showing unsuspected potentialities of the dream of Jesus.

4. Christianity and the churches

Soon two large ecclesial formations took shape in history, the Roman Catholic Church in the West and the Orthodox Church in the East. There are still other smaller churches like the Melkite, the Coptic, and others. These two major formations have their own characteristics derived primarily from the ways of life of the surrounding cultures. The Western church fell strongly under the influence of Roman law and the imperial palace bureaucracy, and hence it is more centralized and strongly structured around the figure of Christ-*Pantokrator;* the Eastern church developed more autonomously, with the different patriarchates, whose exercise of power resembles that of the Middle Eastern satrapies, but in a spiritual rather than juridical sense. The power of the Christian message is located in solemn and lengthy liturgical celebrations centered around the eucharist and emphasizing the figure of the

Risen Christ, the Holy Spirit, and Mary, who are incarnated, as it were, in the wonderful icons that fill the churches and the homes of the faithful. Social engagement is minimal because they regard it the duty of the state to assure that society works properly, while the church handles the care of souls. Both churches are regarded as the "lungs" by which Christianity breathes. Unfortunately, they split in 1054, especially over the doctrine of the procession of the Holy Spirit *(filioque)*, and the claim of jurisdictional primacy by the bishop of Rome. A schism was created, but it did not affect the substance of the faith, because both assumed the christological and trinitarian doctrines of the first five ecumenical councils.

In the sixteenth century the Protestant Reformation led to the emergence of various evangelical churches, especially with Hus, Luther, Zwingli, and Calvin. They all sought to proclaim a gospel purified of the historical and doctrinal distortions that had arisen in the Roman Catholic Church. Subsequently, a plethora of Christian denominations has arisen around the world, each trying to take on the totality of the legacy of Jesus and to live it in widely varying cultural contexts. The phenomenon of Pentecostal and charismatic churches, both evangelical and Catholic, is strong. Both regard the Holy Spirit as the source of inspiration. They have brought creativity and joy into communities previously centered on the cross, and they have broken the monopoly of the word maintained by the hierarchy. However, they have proven not very sensitive to historic conflicts, the issue of social justice, and the real liberation of the oppressed. In them, the "our Father" prevails too strongly over "our bread," a unity sought by Jesus in his dream of the reign.

However, it would be simplistic to interpret the emergence of this ecclesial pluralism as tearing apart the seamless garment of Christ. Viewed positively, they represent different ways of historically embodying the legacy of Jesus. The only vice that contaminates a large portion of these churches, including especially the Roman Catholic Church, is each one's claim to be better than the others, when it is not the only true and exclusive bearer of the dream of Jesus. The aim of ecumenism is that the churches all recognize one another mutually so that together they may present more convincingly and brightly the profoundly human and divine message of Jesus. The four Gospels serve as the reference point for true ecumenism, for while they are different they recognize one another mutually as authentic and give witness to the sole living Gospel that is Jesus. Or consider faith in the Blessed Trinity, in which there is diversity of Persons, all equally infinite and eternal but accepting one another in love and communion so deeply that they are one sole God. Why should it be different with the churches? In their differences and uniquenesses they make up the church of Jesus and the church of God on earth. The diversity of ecclesial communities finds a likeness in the biodiversity of nature.

5. Christianity at the mercy of sacred and political power

The Roman Catholic Church has followed a unique path that we now pause to consider in some detail, because it is the one in which we are members and because it is the largest. In order to better understand its present historical configuration, we must take into account the two axes that have shaped it: one political, the idea of the Roman Empire, and the other theological, the idea of Saint Augustine's (354–430) *City of God*. From the Roman Empire it inherited the sense of law, hierarchy, bureaucracy, and the imperial perspective of conquering all peoples to the Christian message. From Saint Augustine it assumed the idea that it represents the City of God over against the city of men, where sin and Satan rule. The church is the small reconciled world uncontaminated by the city of man. The fact is, however, that this imagined reconciled world is permeated by the city of men, with its vanities, vices, and sins. Just as the church may never be identified with the reign of God, the City of God will never be fully achieved. Both cities are mixed within it, and the existence of a church continually in need of conversion and purification becomes dramatic.

However, through historical circumstances foreign to its own nature, the institutional church was asked to play a role of political power in the Roman Empire, which was in an advanced phase of decline. This began after 325 CE with the emperor Constantine. The church was officially installed as a politico-religious institution in 392 CE when Theodosius the Great (d. 395) made Christianity the official religion of the state. With the Byzantine emperor Justinian I (483–565)—who was to unite West and East and reconquer North Africa and even draw up the first legal code based on Christian faith, the Code of Justinian (520)—Christianity was made obligatory for all. Other religions were persecuted, prohibited, and even wiped out. Yesterday's persecuted became today's persecutors. The martyrs on one side, Christians, produced martyrs on the other side, pagans. Since then the church institution has assumed this power with all its titles, honors, pomp, and palace ways, which has lasted to this day in the manner of life of bishops, cardinals, and popes. This mode of being frequently scandalizes the faithful, who come from reading the Gospels, where they discover the poor and humble Nazarene, close to the people and far from palaces and temples. It is the price that has to be paid: losing the simple poor folk who end up not being evangelized or simply turned into a mass, consuming symbolic goods.

The key category shaping the Roman Catholic Church is *potestas sacra*, sacred power. This power is top down and exercised by a specialized body, clergy, headed by the pope, supreme bearer of sacred power. Over time this power took on ever more centralized forms, sometimes displaying totalitarian or even tyrannical characteristics. Saint Bernard (d. 1153), for example, even writes to Pope Eugenius III (d. 1153) that he is "more a successor of Constantine than of Peter." This tendency became even more pronounced with Pope Gregory VII (d. 1085) in 1075, especially in his decree *Dictatus Papae*. He proclaims himself absolute lord over the secular world, subjecting kings and emperors to his approval, installing and removing them as he sees fit. Along the same line of radicalization, Innocent III (d. 1216), the most powerful pope in history, since all Europe and even Russia were subject to him through pacts of suzerainty, presented himself as not only successor of Peter but representative of Christ. Then Innocent IV (d. 1254), still not satisfied, took the final step and claimed to be representative of God and hence universal lord over the earth. Endowed with this divine power, the popes arrogated to themselves the right to distribute portions of the earth to whomever they wished, as indeed happened. Through the Treaty of Tordesillas, the popes divided the world to be conquered between Spain and Portugal. With the bull *Romanus Pontifex*, Pope Nicholas V (d. 1455) granted Portugal a half, and with the bull *Inter Caetera* Pope Alexander VI (d. 1503) gave the other half to Spain. All that was lacking was to proclaim the pope infallible, and that happened in 1870, with Vatican I under Pius IX. The pope was said to enjoy absolute power: "ordinary, supreme, full, immediate and universal" (canon 331), attributes actually applicable only to God. Indeed, some theologians, sycophants of the popes, called them *deus minor in terra*, that is, the lesser god on earth.

6. Christianity subjected to the pathologies of power

Now that the topic is power, a comparison between two attitudes, that of Jesus and that of the Roman Catholic Church with regard to power, is germane. They are at odds. The evangelists present power under the form of three diabolic temptations (Mk 1:12–13; Mt 4:1–11; Lk 4:1–13). They are placed right after the beginning of the Gospels, before Jesus' preaching, as a kind of warning and an introduction so that hearers will understand Jesus' intention correctly. He is indeed the Messiah, but different, deprived of any power, and made Suffering Servant. The temptations display the three classic forms of power: the *prophetic*, of effective words that turn stones into bread; the *priestly*, which reforms customs starting from the temple; the *political*, which dominates peoples and creates empires. Jesus is confronted with these powers presented by Satan as projects that he is to choose. Jesus firmly rejects all three. His way is not that of the Messiah that many expected, who wields all these powers, but that of the Suffering Servant and of the Persecuted Prophet proclaimed by Isaiah (53). This is the basic core of the preaching of the Gospels. With the church, a huge hierarchical organization, what has happened is just the opposite. Confronted with these three temptations, it has not been able to resist; it has succumbed to all of them dramatically. It has assumed the *prophetic* power of the word, monopoly of the authorities, and control over miracles; *priestly* power, exercised in a centralized way in the figure of the pope, and distributed over the clerical body, leaving lay people, men and women, completely out; and *political* power wielded as in an absolute monarchy, embodied in the Vatican state and the figure of the pope. This has occurred especially during the long time when the popes held all power, secular and religious, in their hands, maintaining a papal state, with its bureaucracy, its private central bank, with armies and a justice system that even sentenced people to death. In its basic structure this type of organization remains today, with all the contradictions that it entails. It is hard to escape the criticism Jesus directed at Peter, who did not understand Jesus' path of suffering and was accused of being "a stumbling block" and "a temptation" (Mt 16:23). Jesus would never build his church on the rock of the Vatican the way it is.

Indeed, the history of the papacy reveals great contradictions. We are accustomed to inspiring figures like Pius X, Pius XI, Pius XII, John XXIII, Paul VI, John Paul I, and John Paul II, all of them embodying notable virtues. However, there have been eras of worldly popes in head-on contradiction to the legacy of Peter and of Jesus. The eminent Cardinal Baronius (1538–1607), a historian and Vatican librarian, even speaks of the pornocratic age of the papacy from 900 to around 1000 CE. Thus Pope Sergius (904) murdered his two predecessors; Pope John XII (944), elected when he was twenty years old, an adulterer, was killed by the betrayed husband, and worse yet, Pope Benedict IX (1033), elected at age thirteen, proved to be one of the most criminal and disgraceful popes in history, going so far as to sell the papal dignity for one thousand silver lira. The nadir of the papacy was reached with Pope Stephen VI (896–97), who ordered that his predecessor, Pope Formosus (891–96), be exhumed. His decaying corpse was dressed up in the pontifical vestments and placed on the papal chair. The cardinals appointed by him had to kiss his hand. An ad hoc synod in the presence of the corpse ordered that he be deposed as pope and condemned. The signs of his office were taken away from him, and the fingers of his right hand, used for blessing, were cut off. Finally, his cadaver was handed over to the populace and thrown into the Tiber River. This macabre scene ultimately turned against Stephen VI, who was thrown in prison and finally strangled. These appalling contradictions notwithstanding, the figure of the pope has constituted an ongoing reference point of unity, continuity of the apostolic tradition, and a call to the churches to constitute together the Jesus movement, with a minimal level of mutual acceptance and unity so that Christian witness may gain credibility. The ecumenical problem lies not in the fact of the papacy but in the centralized authoritarian way that it is exercised, leaving little room for the legitimate differences found in the other Christian churches.

The price to be paid by a hierarchical church institution that is built on power is living constantly in disputes, conflicts, crusades, and wars with other wielders of power, now aligned with them, now deposing them from their throne and excommunicating them, always seeking more power. A church institution of power closes the door to love and loses the poor. Allied with the powerful, it becomes incapable of evangelizing the marginalized and the workers, who form the mass of the faithful and are held in submission with no participation in the decisions related to the church's life and organization. The poor are seen from the standpoint of the rich, so always needy and the object of charity and assistance. Workers are seen from the standpoint of the employer, always under submission and turned into fuel for the production process. Rarely are the poor seen with the eyes of the poor so as to recognize their power in history, capable of being an alternative to the dominant society, and therefore with the power to transform history. Likewise, workers are seldom seen from the side of workers, their labor unions, and their ability to set limits to the voraciousness of capital, and so as an agent for another kind of society, one that is more equal and just. When these large majorities are marginalized from the institution, the dream of Jesus is distanced, becomes worldly, loses its human countenance, and becomes insensitive to existential problems, often enough showing itself cruel and merciless toward issues related to family and sexuality.

In culture as a whole, the church institution became a bastion of authoritarianism, conservativism, and machismo, ever more distant from the course of the world, finding it very difficult to establish an honest and open dialogue with realities other than itself. Its institutional arrogance of being the sole bearer and legitimate interpreter of revelation, of being the only true church of Christ, denying the title church to everyone else but the Orthodox, and presenting itself as the sole bearer of the means of salvation to the point of repeating the medieval teaching "outside the church no salvation," becomes ever more unacceptable to people with common sense, an ecumenical religious spirit, and a minimum of theological culture. It is in danger of becoming a huge Western Christian sect. But it has to be recognized that despite the narrowness of the institutional framework, there have arisen prophetic and holy shepherds who have taken on the cause of the poor and the oppressed, as has happened far and wide in the Latin American church. Lay men and women, outstanding in their intelligence and knowledge, have made their faith a political force for social transformation. Many of them have been victims of violence from their own brethren in the faith and from social groups, most of them Catholic, more interested in defending their privileges than in fostering the observance of rights.

Efforts to convert this authoritarian type of hierarchical church, made by the Reformation in the sixteenth century and by Vatican II in the twentieth century (1962–65), shifting the accents from sacred power to sacred service, from the hierarchy to the people of God, from the church building closed in on itself to the church with its doors and windows open to dialogue with modernity, with the other churches and religions, have been frustrated and nullified by the Vatican bureaucracy, legitimized by popes John Paul II and Benedict XVI. They have reassumed and reinforced a model of church with medieval features, reintroducing Latin in masses following the sixteenth-century rite of Pius V; they have treated with kid gloves the schismatic followers of Archbishop Lefebvre but used clubs on those allied with the poor, the liberation bishops and theologians. They have headed toward restoration and the return to the great discipline. The aim is obvious: fortify the system of sacred, single-sex (only men), celibate, priestly, centralized, authoritarian, hierarchical, and exclusive power. This conception of power and its exercise can scarcely fit into Jesus' utopia of power as service and never as hierarchy (sacred power).

7. Christianity from the side of the people

Alongside the official version of Christianity embodied in learned Greco-Latin-Germanic-modern culture there arose from the beginning a vigorous popular Christianity, especially in the peripheral churches but also in the central churches, as may be found in Europe generally, but more clearly in Italy and Spain. It isn't a decadent form of the official form; on the contrary, it has equal dignity since it embodies Jesus' message in the people's worldview. It is not so much *logos* as *pathos* that organizes its discourses. It is expressed in the language of imagination, heart, and feeling. It has its truths and its way of speaking, of praying to God, and living the dream of Jesus. This kind of popular Christianity has almost always been disdained, and the faithful have been subjected to the doctrines and rites of the clerical body. Without confronting and directly entering in conflict with the official model, it has created its own path and developed a Christianity of daily life, personal and family virtues, following Jesus, usually crucified, in whom the people see their own crucified situation. These anonymous people, whose guiding archetype is Saint Joseph, have kept the secret of the dream of Jesus, made up of hope, of many personal and family virtues, and of a trusting surrender to God's will. Outside of power, they have not suffered the pathologies proper to the bearers of power, such as careerism, flattery, dual morality, legalism, hypocrisy, hardness of heart, and arrogance. They live a pure and simple Christianity, the authentic heirs of the ethic of Jesus and of his dream, of a world where the goods of the reign begin, and the divine promises are anticipated. As in all things, they have their limits and their mistakes. Often enough their Christianity mixes trusting faith with superstition, it engages in a syncretism that does not always work well, and it too easily supernaturalizes natural events and sees them as miracles. But as illnesses lead back to health, likewise here such deviations lead back to the substance of the gospel of Jesus with its full charge of hope and the joy that it radiates. Popular Christianity is festive, accompanied by protective male and female saints, and full of color, dancing, and food and drink.

8. Christianity and its reductionisms

Any incarnation of Christianity in cultures means embodiment but also limitation and reduction. How much of the dream of Jesus, his practice, his message, and his ethic does the Greco-Roman-Western paradigm carry? It incorporates Christianity within its possibilities, but at the cost of notable limitations and regrettable reductions. It is important to liberate the root experience of Jesus and lessen the institutional arrogance of the Roman Catholic Church, which claims to present the entire legacy of Jesus with no reductionism and no relativism, and even worse, condemns the reductionisms of others without taking notice of its own. Hence, we need to proceed to a critical reflection. The issue isn't reductionism. That belongs to any process of incarnation; it isn't a defect but a mark of history. The issue is being blind to that fact and presenting oneself as someone who hasn't reduced anything, confusing the part with the whole, as if its real but unconscious reductionism were the entirety of the gospel and the dream of Jesus. Let us list some of these reductionisms, for in that way we will free Christianity of this pathology so that it can unimpededly carry out other future attempts at incarnation.

Instead of preaching the *Trinity*-God, Roman Catholic Christianity remained with Old Testament pre-trinitarian monotheism. The doctrine of a single God, prevalent in sermons and in theological reflection itself, was and is better suited to a culture of authoritarian power and unified thought prevailing in patriarchal culture.

Instead of extending the *dream of Jesus*, the reign of God, it proclaims the church, outside of which there is no salvation, often in alliance with the powerful, and far away from the poor and oppressed.

Instead of preaching the *resurrection* as the greatest event in history, a true *tremendum,* in the language of Pierre Teilhard de Chardin, it has tended to proclaim the immortality of the soul, a Platonic belief widely popularized in Roman, Greek, and Western cultures.

Instead of presenting the *real Jesus of history*, it opted for a Jesus defined in philosophical and theological terms from the councils of Nicea (325), Constantinople (381), Ephesus (431), and Chalcedon (451) as it appears in the current creed. There he is professed as "God from God, Light from Light, true God from true God, begotten not made, consubstantial with as the Father." Then it is said that he "became man. For our sake he was crucified under Pontius Pilate, he suffered death and was buried." Nothing is said about his life, message, work, and why he was killed. Basically, all it says is that "he was born and he died." This is a reductionism that utterly empties out the human reality of Jesus, that which really matters, without recognizing the very great danger of hollowing out the Mystery of the incarnation.

Instead of strengthening the *community,* in which all shared in all, it introduced the hierarchy of persons and division of functions, creating two bodies in the churches, the clerical body, which knows everything and can do everything, and the lay body, which is simply supposed to hear and execute.

Instead of the *communion of goods*, a defining feature of the early Christian communities, attested by the Acts of the Apostles (chaps. 2, 4), there has prevailed the individualist spirit by which each lives for himself or herself, each strives to save his or her own soul.

But there is a second kind of reductionism, this one even deeper, which affects the substance of the newness brought by Jesus. The root experience of Christianity of *God as Trinity of Persons*, ever in perichoresis, mutual communion of life and love, has not been able to prevail historically. This fundamental and original intuition, as compared with the other religions, was soon captured by disputes deriving from the Greek paradigm of thought. For the most part it is characterized by a substantialist, identity focus, as opposed to a process view of life and history, not very suited for conceiving the Trinity as a play of relationships among the three Divine Persons. By its very nature the Trinity demands another paradigm, one that views reality in constant process of realization and of emergence as is proper of Mystery—as we have pondered previously—and typical of phenomena like life, nature, and spirit. Most Christian thinkers, incapable of grasping the uniqueness of the Christian way of saying God, have kept the pastoral discourse of the churches within classic pre-trinitarian monotheism common to Judaism and the religions of the world. The Blessed Trinity has remained the symbol of the Mystery of Mysteries and hence regarded as inaccessible to human reason and the object of pure faith. Efforts at deepening within the confines of the Greek *logos* have produced intricate arguments with countless heresies, thereby isolating even further this truth of the life and practice of Christians. It remained present in the liturgy more ritually than existentially.

Another reductionism has to do with the *eclipse of the figure of the Father as Father of the Son.* In the Creed he is professed to be "the Father Almighty, maker of heaven and earth," all-knowing and supreme judge, absolute Lord of life and death. Alongside such a Father there remains no room for a Son, and so he is not lived trinitarianly as Father of the Son, but as Creator of all things. This religion of the Father has served and is still serving as ideological justification of all kinds of paternalism and authoritarianism by which people are kept in dependency and servility. One Father in heaven, God; one father on earth, the monarch or president; one father in the church, the pope; one father in the community, the head; and one father in the family, the father as maximum authority. This is still the prevailing representation.

Excessive exaltation of the figure of the Son. Obliviousness of the trinitarian vision has led to an exaggerated concentration on the figure of the Son incarnate in Jesus Christ. *Christomonism* (exclusive predominance of Christ) has emerged, as though Christ were the sole and exclusive reality, and there were no Father and Holy Spirit together with him. He is seen as the sole universal Savior, a liberating leader, solitary, adored with all the symbols of power, always exalted as Lord and "Christokrator," having the scepter in one hand, the world in the other, and a jeweled golden crown on his head, something that the historic Jesus may never have seen with his own eyes; he would indignantly refuse to be adorned with such regalia. The figure of suffering servant and human traveling companion, the Christ of the traveling couple of Emmaus, is powerfully eclipsed. The exaggeration of the figure of Christ, indivisible head of the visible church, bolsters the authoritarian figures and institutions rooted in centralizing power. This type of reductionist Christology has created its compensatory opposite, which is the youth Christology prepared for young people. There Jesus is portrayed as a handsome and enthusiastic leader and a vigorous hero, as though just coming out of a gym, to be followed and exalted. But this Hollywood image is almost always disconnected from the conflicts inherent in life and history. And then in romantic terms there emerges a Jesus of the family apostolate, presented between Mary and Joseph, or as the sweet Jesus of Nazareth blessing children, or as the good shepherd, surrounded by sheep in lush green pastures, or sadly looking at the city of Jerusalem, which has rejected him. A religion of the Son alone is enclosed on itself as if nothing existed beyond itself. It becomes incapable of seeing the presence of the Spirit and the values of the reign in spiritual paths that are not Christian, and is a short step away from exclusivism and fundamentalism with regard to revelation and salvation.

The third reductionism has to do with *forgetting the figure of the Holy Spirit*. It was only late in theological reflection that the Holy Spirit was admitted as Third Person of the Trinity, and it was held hostage in theological disputes between Orthodoxy and the Latin church in relation to *filioque*, that is, the relationship of origin of the Spirit. Is he spirated solely by the Father, as the Son is generated (Orthodoxy), or is he spirated by the Father *and by the* Son, or *through* the Son (the *filioque* of the Latin church)? This theological argument, which deep down seems irrelevant, in fact conceals power disputes between the two poles of Christendom, the West and the East, and has split the two fundamental churches until our own time. The upshot has been a shift; the churches have come in to occupy the place of the Spirit. He ended up having a lateral and secondary function. Whether the churches like it or not, the Spirit is the source of creativity and innovation, blows where it will, and goes out ahead of the missionary, for it becomes present in peoples through love, forgiveness, and shared life and solidarity. However, the institutions see the Spirit as a factor disturbing the established order and therefore put it off to the side and even forget it. As a result of this conservative and reductionist understanding, men and women of the Spirit, mystics and founders of new spiritual paths, have always had difficulty in being recognized by the ecclesiastical institution, which has kept them, and still keeps them, under harsh surveillance, when it does not marginalize or even condemn them. They forget Paul's harsh warning: "Do not stifle the Spirit" (1 Thes 5:19). An ecclesial community without the conscious presence of the Spirit is generally dominated by ossified and bureaucratic ecclesiastical authorities, clutching order and power. On the other hand, charismatic movements that seek to nourish a personal experience of God find in the Holy Spirit their source of inspiration. That serves to explain the spread of grassroots charismatic churches, whether evangelical or Catholic, with very similar forms of piety and organization. This charismatic expression has helped spread the word in the church, otherwise reserved solely to the hierarchy, and has opened space for ritual and symbolic creativity, previously denied by the canonical rigidity of the official liturgy. But it clearly suffers from shortcomings by not connecting issues of injustice, the poor, and social transformation to the gospel and the creativity proper to the Spirit. Hence, a religion solely of the Spirit easily falls into sentimentalism, youthful enthusiasm, and alienation in relation to the conflictive aspect of life; it may even end in fanaticism and spiritual anarchy.

To this day Christendom has never found a balance point with regard to the *assumption of the Divine Persons* as the true God of the Christian experience. It has become far removed from its originating identity of a God of love and communion, which ought to be expressed in history with behaviors and initiatives to foster community, with equal participation of all, and the understanding of Christianity as something that is ever open to new manifestations in widely varying cultures. That was not primarily what prevailed. Things were turned ridiculously upside down in the Roman Catholic Church: what was true in the doctrine of the Trinity (absence of hierarchy, since all the Divine Persons are equally eternal, infinite, and omnipotent) becomes heresy in the church (there is no equality among Christians, but a hierarchy of men alone, supposedly willed by God, and an essential difference between clerics and lay people).

9. The future of Christianity in the age of globalization

What does the future hold for this type of Latin, Western, and outmoded church at our time in history? That depends on what the future holds for the Western culture that it has helped shape. Surely the future of humankind will no longer go through the West, which is increasingly becoming incidental.

Today the majority presence of Christianity is in the Third and Fourth Worlds. Despite the control exercised by the Vatican central authorities, we have here a vigorous new attempt to incarnate Christianity in the various cultures. Christianity as a whole will have significance only under two conditions: if all the churches mutually recognize one another as bearers of the message of Jesus, with none of them raising the claim of being exclusive and exceptional, and out of this "perichoresis" (inter-retro-relations) of the churches engage in dialogue with the world religions and accept one another as spiritual paths where the Spirit is present and at work. That is the only way to religious peace, which is one of the major prior conditions for world peace. The second condition is that Christianity be demythologized, de-Westernized, and de-patriarchialized, and become organized in networks of communities that dialogue with, and become incarnate in, local cultures, mutually accept one another, and together form the great Christian spiritual path that joins together with the other spiritual and religious paths of humankind. All will feed the sacred flame of the presence of the Trinity-God in the heart of each person and in the universe. Christianity will help people to be reconnected to nature, to Mother Earth, and to God-communion. Then Christianity will be able humbly to present itself in its uniqueness as one among other sources of reconnecting among human beings, among peoples, with nature, with earth, and with God, Source of all life, of all meaning, and of all love. It will be through their witness to the resurrection begun in Jesus that they will nourish the hope of a magnificent end for the universe.

10. Christianity and its civilizing contribution

These reductionisms notwithstanding, it must be recognized that this type of incarnation has made a priceless contribution to the political consciousness of the West, and from there to the whole world: the inviolable dignity of the human person, no matter how poor and lowly he or she might appear. From there have flowed universal rights; the ideals of equality, liberty, and fraternity; and the very idea of democracy. As nature was "de-divinized," it was freed and could be studied by science and transformed by technology, although it has not been able with its preaching and catechesis to imbue the kind of respect necessary so that technology and science, carried out with conscience and ethical sense, serve not solely for the aims of accumulation and the market but for life and the preservation of everything created.

Christianity has been best expressed where it has been lived and is still being lived as spirituality, that is, as a journey seeking perfection by cultivating love for God; for neighbor, especially the forgotten and the last; and for all things in creation. This spirituality is governed less by doctrines than by listening to the Spirit, who speaks through the signs of the times, through personal encounter with the Risen Christ, who permeates all matter and history, and by following his way of life in history. From the outset, and even with veiled critique of the imperial church, there emerged everywhere, beginning in Egypt and Syria, the monastic movement of anchorites, cenobites, and even stylites. Monastic religious life started in the sixth century with Saint Benedict. The various orders and congregations emerged, notably among the mendicants, with Saint Dominic, Saint Francis, and the Servites in the twelfth century. In modern times there are the Little Brothers and Sisters of Charles de Foucauld, who became entranced by the figure and gospel message of Jesus humble and poor. They have been characterized by a strong spirituality, and the Christian virtues have been cultivated to a noteworthy degree. The values of the reign are particularly incarnated in those religious women and men who have surrendered their lives to the poor and oppressed, to the disinherited of this world, to those abandoned in the forests, serving them generously, often risking their lives, and even being martyred for the sake of the rights of the poor and the greater justice of the reign. Or like Mother Teresa of Calcutta, who picked up the dying from the streets so that they could die with dignity, surrounded by people and prayers.

These exemplary figures have made Christianity credible and have attested that the reign is under way and that its goods can make history even in the midst of great contradictions. The Christian mystics are exemplary figures of spiritual life. In them the reign of God has been intensely and effectively anticipated. It is they who are and have been those who have most experienced the Trinity-God, such as Saint John of the Cross, Saint Teresa of Avila, Meister Eckhart, Saint Francis of Assisi, Saint Bonaventure, Saint Francis de Sales, Blessed Angela of Foligno, Pierre Teilhard de Chardin, and Thomas Merton, among so many men and women, most of them anonymous but filled with the Spirit of God.

If there is a field in which Christianity has shown its beauty and unsuspected depth it has been in the field of celebration. Christians know how to celebrate the paschal mystery and the life and work of Jesus. They have created powerful symbols and music, such as Gregorian chant, whose beauty touches the depth of the soul, and the polyphonic masses that raise us to the heavens and arouse such sublime feelings that the Blessed Trinity becomes present and its grace may be savored. Many feasts and celebrations have taken root in Christian life, such as the rituals of Holy Week, Christmas, Easter, Pentecost, and Corpus Christi, the great pilgrimages of Canindé and Aparecida do Norte in Brazil, Our Lady of Guadalupe in Mexico, Lourdes in France, Fatima in Portugal, and the biblical sites in Israel.

Another field of expression of Christianity, one of the purest and most beautiful, has been music. We can say that there has never been any significant conflict between Christianity and music. Music and experience of the sacred, melody and celebration of the presence of Mystery, have a similar nature. How can we not be affected by Bach's Saint Matthew Passion, his Magnificat, his fugues? Mozart's Requiem, the melodious work of Palestrina, the grave and solemn masses of Father José Mauricio in the time of the empire? North American black spirituals, the songs of great melodic beauty and liberating message of the Christian base communities? The *Misa Campesina* of Nicaragua, the masses of the Terra Sem males and of the Quilombos [hidden slave communities in Brazil], the great black singer Milton Nascimento and Bishop Pedro Casaldáliga, the prophet of the oppressed minorities, among so many other musical works of different genres?

The values of Christianity have found a most fertile field of expression in art. Let us think especially of the centuries-old cathedrals, the majestic churches in the West and the East; church buildings of the most varied styles, from the simplicity of Romanesque art, through the transcendental height of the Gothic, to the profusion of colors and statues of the Baroque, and the light and stylized iconic modern art of the materials of the cathedral in Brasilia. Painting and sculpture have found inspiration in Jesus and the Christian mysteries producing works of unsurpassable beauty such as the Sistine Chapel, the statues of the Pietà and Moses of Michelangelo, the Last Supper and the Mona Lisa of Leonardo da Vinci, the prophets of Aleijadinho, the mysterious icons of Orthodoxy, especially Russian and Greek, the indigenous-Latin American-Christian syncretism of churches and statuary in Mexico, Ecuador, Peru, Brazil, and elsewhere. African, Chinese, and Japanese religious sculptures are of unique and incomparable beauty. In this realm Christianity has shown an elevating power of matchless spirituality. Popular Christianity has contributed with artistic forms in sculpture and painting of great quality and creativity, with a naivete that takes us back to the earthly paradise before its fall. The effect of Christianity in literature, in poetry and novels, has been just as great. There is a tradition of great sacred orators, from the most widely known, like Saint Augustine, Saint Leo the Great, and Saint Gregory I, to Lacordaire, Bossuet, Saint Leonard of Port-Maurice, and Padre Antonio Vieira, a classic in the Portuguese language. How can one fail to mention the *Divine Comedy* of Dante Alighieri, where Christian poetry reached a still unsurpassed height and beauty? The entire work of Ernesto Cardenal, especially his superb *Canto Cósmico*, and the many writings of Alceu Amoroso Lima (Tistão de Athayde) and of Carlos Alberto Libânio Christo (Frei Betto), imbued with mysticism and a refined literary beauty, to mention only some names. We may also think of some notable writers who have dealt with the Christian legacy like Goethe, Thomas Mann, Paul Claudel, Cervantes, Fernando Pessoa, and Machado de Assis, among so many other men and women. The same could be said of remarkable filmmakers from many lands.

Christianity opened theoretical space for the scientific project of modernity by secularizing the world and thus making it an object of investigation. Initially, there was a conflict between the classic worldview held by the Roman hierarchy, which was overcome by religious figures like Copernicus and Pascal. Geniuses like Newton, Francis Bacon, philosophers like Kant, Hegel, Nietzsche, Heidegger, and indeed Marx-Engels, or sociologists and analysts like Max Weber and Gramsci, among so many others who could not be understood without their critical contact with Christianity. Remarkable politicians have drawn ethical and humanistic inspiration from Christian faith, like Adenauer in Germany, DeGaspari and Della Pira in Italy, DeGaulle in France, Kennedy in the United States, Mariategui in Peru, and Lula in Brazil.

Finally, Christianity has made its way into the world of virtual images. It has inspired countless films on the life of Christ, his passion, and his Mystery. Others have taken up matters related to Christianity such as the missions, the lives of the saints, documentaries on the holy places, and sacred art. Here Christianity has attained a prominence unknown in the past and has emerged as a part of planetary awareness. Only today has it attained a quantitative catholicity, reaching practically all the most distant reaches of the earth. The Internet has opened the way for an unimaginable spread of the Christian message, whose effects are still beyond comprehension.

0.10. d archetypal figures who in their lives have witnessed to the transforming and humanizing power of the dream of Jesus and of his way of being; they are the proclaimers of the gospel of the various churches, the humble preachers among the people in the most distant and inhospitable places, religious men and women serving in the poorest slums, in hospitals, and leper colonies. They are also, on the Catholic side, saints, martyrs, confessors, and virgins who attest that the seed of the reign scattered by Jesus has not remained sterile; rather, falling on fertile ground, it has sprouted and flourished. The most generous spirits of the West were gestated in Christian space due to the goods of the reign, which have never ceased fermenting in history. Shining brightly in their intelligence have been geniuses like Origen, Saint Augustine, Saint Irenaeus, medieval masters like Saint Thomas Aquinas, Saint Bonaventure, Duns Scotus, William of Ockham; in the fifteenth and sixteenth century, Hus, Luther, Zwingli, Calvin, Melanchthon, Bartolomé de las Casas; and in modern times, Schleiermacher, Karl Barth, Rudolf Bultmann, Jürgen Moltmann, Karl Rahner, Dietrich Bonheoffer; and in our circles, Gustavo Gutiérrez, Juan Luis Segundo, Hugo Assmann, Jon Sobrino, and Paulo Freire. The mystics have already been mentioned, but the most noteworthy are those anonymous people who have shaped their lives in the light of the life of Jesus of Nazareth, the Christ of faith, such as our grandparents, parents, relatives, and so many other people around us. Some have become Christian and even universal landmarks, such as the Christian martyrs thrown to the wild beasts in the Roman arenas for the entertainment of the masses. Later there arose figures like Saint Francis of Assisi and Saint Clare; Father Damien and Albert Schweitzer, both committed to caring for lepers; Saint Vincent de Paul, caring for those lying in the street; John Wesley in England, serving the workers; Martin Luther King Jr., struggling for the civil rights of blacks; Bartolomé de las Casas, saving the indigenous of Mesoamerica from the barbarism of European colonizers; Pope John XXIII, who opened the doors and windows of the old church institution to the world of today; Archbishop Oscar Romero of El Salvador, martyred while celebrating the Eucharist, mixing his blood with the consecrated blood of Christ, shot dead by an assassin's bullet; the Jesuit martyrs of El Salvador, sacrificed because they defended the dignity of the least and oppressed; Dom Hélder Câmara, bishop of the poor, and perhaps the greatest prophet of the Third World in the twentieth century; Mother Teresa of Calcutta, creating conditions so that those dying in the streets could die with dignity; Blessed Sister Dulce Pontes, taking care of the marginalized who lived in houses on stilts in Salvador de Bahia; Sister Dorothy Stang, murdered for defending the Amazon forest and impoverished peoples.

Missionaries merit special mention. It is true that many of them went *ad gentes* with a conquest mindset, alongside the colonial powers. But regardless of the questionable theologies circulating in their heads, they threw themselves into the hell of dire poverty, in the heart of harsh tropical forests, in the most abject outlying areas, ever seeking to serve the life of people, and at the same time caring for their adhesion to the gospel. Many have been persecuted, calumniated, abused, imprisoned, tortured, and murdered for the cause for which they courageously left their homelands, their families, and their cultures of origin, and devoted lives to others. They make up the multitude of those marked by the blood of the Lamb (Rv 7:13) and are in God's heart and in the perpetual memory of Christians and of humankind. The list of these witnesses to the gospel is endless. It is they who have given Christianity credibility; they have shown that the assassination of Christ was not in vain, and that the dream of a reign of justice, love, mercy, solidarity, and peace, despite opposition from the empire of the negative, continues to germinate within history, pushing it toward its happy conclusion. Rather than ideas, messages, doctrines, and dogmas, it is lives that convince and lead people to approach that Source which nourishes these seminal Christians and all those who live in love, justice, and solidarity toward those who are last.

Conclusion

Et tunc erit finis
(All is consummated)

What is Christianity? It isn't Christ continued. It is something else, but it can't be understood without Christ. The former, Christ, is the Mystery of the Son, who was incarnated. The latter, Christianity, is an event in history open and still in construction, based on the reign of God, which did not come in fullness but was made possible by the failure of the cross and by the victory that was the partial implementation of this reign through the resurrection of Jesus.

What will happen to that reign? It will be that which it is allowed to achieve in history, inspired by the deeds of Jesus and in connection with the history of peoples. But both Jesus and history have something in common; they emerge out of the evolutionary process. Christ as the self-communication of the Son of the Father to a specific man, Jesus of Nazareth, and at the same time also the complete openness of the specific man, Jesus, to the Son of the Father. He is the sacrament of encounter. Both movements cross in him: internalization with externalization, the ascending with the descending movement. Jesus accordingly represents the seminal anticipation of the final condition of humankind and the universe, assumed and internalized by the Holy Spirit, by the Son, and by the Father, and brought into the reign of the Trinity, but this has only been possible because the Son first entered and was externalized in the world through the action of the Spirit under the aegis of the Father and became our humanity.

In this sense, restricting ourselves only to Jesus, he represents a glory of God and an honor for us and for the entire universe, but he also bears a tragedy that represents the *crux theologorum*. He was rejected and executed on the cross. This fate resulted from what he said and what he did, which was unacceptable to the political and religious standards of the time. Jesus did not seek death, nor was it desired by the Father. Jesus loved life and hoped for the realization of his dream, the reign. What the Father wanted was not the death of the Son, for the Father isn't cruel. He wanted the Son's fidelity, which could entail violent death. Amid tears, anguish, and cries of desperation, Jesus held to the end onto fidelity to himself, to the dream, to humiliated and wronged men and women, and to the Father. Although he loved life, he had to surrender it and accept death as judicial execution.

In this he didn't fail, for at no time did he betray fidelity. His proposal failed historically because it was rejected. The response to his fidelity was resurrection as the seminal, inchoate, and inaugural realization of his dream: the reign of God. Hence the dream remains a dream, but qualified with this anticipatory sign that is the personal resurrection of Jesus. Since Jesus is never alone but always connected to his community and to the entire universe, his resurrection is still not complete. The Risen Jesus still has a future until everyone and the cosmos itself share in his resurrection and are also resurrected. The Gospels hint at this situation when they insinuate that we are en route to Galilee, where the resurrection still remains to be shown. Galilee is the place where it all began: the manifestation of Jesus and the proclamation of his dream—the imminent reign of God. And Galilee will also be the place where it all ends, when the manifestation of the resurrection will be completed together with the culmination of the evolutionary process with the utter fulfillment of humankind and all creation.

We are still journeying to Galilee, shouting and singing: "Come Lord Jesus, Maranatha," like one awaiting the dawn after a long and stormy night.

Christianity is also an emergence from the universe, whether in the form of the failure of the cross (moment of chaos) or in the form of success (moment of cosmos: generative chaos) that was its incipient resurrection. Everything was reorganized so that the cause of Jesus and the significance of his deeds could be perpetuated in history. The rise of the Jesus movement, the writing of the four Gospels and the other texts of the Second Testament, the founding of communities and of Christian churches in the various cultural regions all show the outward radiation of the figure and message of Jesus over the lives of millions of persons, and also in the arts, music, and written and virtual literature up to our own time. The action of the Christic energies of internalization and externalization are still at work in history. All of this surely was beyond the possible awareness of the Jesus of history, craftsman and peasant. It doesn't matter. It was God who, through him, brought about this emergence in our cosmic, earthly, and human history.

Christianity only has meaning if it keeps alive the awareness that it is an emergence out of the presence of the Son of the Father in our midst, in the power of the Spirit, and in the constant action of the Father. It gains significance to the extent that it does not allow the dream of Jesus to turn cold, keeps the memory of his *verba et facta*, of his glorious and tragic deeds, and tries to make real the dream in things said to be of the reign: love, forgiveness, justice, care for the poor, and complete surrender to *Abba*-Father. One is felt to be in the palm of the Father's hand. The things of the reign manage to arouse in persons the awareness that they are, actually not metaphorically, sons and daughters of the Father, and hence brothers and sisters of one another. Can there be a greater dignity than this, that of knowing we are members of the divine family and of likewise being God, by participation?

Without the presence and activity of the Spirit, Jesus and the history that he set in motion could not be conceived and understood. It is the Spirit who keeps alive the memory of the life and work of Jesus and arouses the enthusiasm necessary for the cause of the reign. Personalized in Mary, the Spirit will make this woman become especially prominent in the piety of the faithful. She represents the female and maternal face of God. This Spirit signifies the creative and charismatic dimension of the church, preventing it from succumbing to the rigidity of traditions, institutions, doctrines, and rituals. It leavens history, fosters movements for life and liberation of the oppressed, stirs up all kinds of initiatives and dreams of a world according to the great dream of Jesus. Men and women saints, martyrs, witnesses of faith, and all the spiritual life are gifts of the Spirit. It is the Spirit who ensures that the many incarnations of the message of Jesus in different cultures preserve Christian identity, and when they lose their way, serves them as saving compass.

Hovering together with the personalized Spirit and Son is the mysterious figure of the Father, who was joined to the father Joseph. He cares for the entire evolutionary process so that in painful ascent it may implode and explode within the reign of the Trinity. The Blessed Trinity within creation assures, despite all possible vicissitudes, the endurance and eternity of this creation. All that the Trinity-God has one day created, loved, assumed, and internalized in its own reality cannot vanish forever. He is the "sovereign lover of life" (Wis 11:21) and of everything that he has created and divinized.

We are God's and we belong to the family of God. Why fear? Christians are bearers, well or poorly, of this awareness. In the midst of many contradictions and with difficult fidelities and heavy betrayals there is always a numerous group that persists and never ceases believing and hoping that the dream of Jesus can be and is going to be achieved. Strength lies not in adherence to doctrines and fidelity to traditions, but in hope against all hope and in the capacity to arouse it in others. When we reach Galilee, where the resurrection of Jesus will be shown fully and will be completed, then we will cease hoping.

Then, with the resurrection, there will be only love and the celebration of those set free, the poor, all called to become peoples of God (Rv 21:2) within a finally rescued creation, transfigured by the energies of the new heaven and the new earth, made into the temple where we and Trinity-God will dwell for endless ages. All will be joy and feasting, feasting and celebration, celebration and reign of the Trinity.

Et tunc erit finis: and then will be the end, *end* as completion of the whole evolutionary process toward Mystery; *end* as goal achieved, after a torturous billion-year rise, interiorization, and externalization; and *end* as culmination of all things in the reign of the Trinity.

Now all that remains is to say a final amen and proclaim that "all is good."

Bibliography

This book is based on the historical, theological, and exegetical research in the following publications by the author:

O Evangelio do Cristo cósmico [The gospel of the cosmic Christ]. Petropolis: Vozes, 1971/2009.

Jesus Christ Liberator: A Critical Christology for Our Time. Maryknoll, NY: Orbis Books, 1978. *Jesus Cristo libertador.* 20th edition. Petropolis: Vozes, 2009.

Passion of Christ, Passion of the World. Maryknoll, NY: Orbis Books, 1987, 2001. *Paixão de Cristo, paixão do mundo.* 6th edition. Petropolis: Vozes, 2007.

A ressurreição na morte [Resurrection in death]. 6th edition. Petropolis: Vozes, 2004.

Natal: a humanidade e a jovialidade de nosso Deus [Christmas: The humanity and joyfulness of our God]. Petropolis: Vozes, 2003.

Way of the Cross, Way of Justice. Maryknoll, NY: Orbis Books, 1980. *Via-sacra da justiça.* 4th ed. Petropolis: Vozes, 1978.

A cross nossa de cada dia [Our daily cross]. Campinas: Verus, 2003.

Trinity and Society. Maryknoll NY: Orbis Books 1988. *A Trindade a sociedade e a libertação.* 5th edition. Petropolis: Vozes, 1999.

Holy Trinity, Perfect Community. Maryknoll, NY: Orbis Books, 2000. *A Santíssima Trindade é a melhor comunidade,* 22nd edition. Petropolis: Vozes, 2009.

The Maternal Face of God: The Feminine and Its Religious Manifestations. San Francisco: Harper and Row, 1987. *O rostro materno de Deus,* 10th edition. Petropolis: Vozes, 2008.

The Lord's Prayer: The Prayer of Integral Liberation. Maryknoll, NY: Orbis Books, 1983. *O Pai-nosso,* 12th edition. Petropolis: Vozes, 2009.

Praying with Jesus and Mary: Our Father, Hail Mary. Maryknoll, NY: Orbis Books, 2005. *A Ave-Maria—O feminino e o Espírito Santo,* 9th edition. Petropolis: Vozes, 2009.

Church, Charism, and Power: Liberation Theology and the Institutional Church. New York: Crossroad, 1985. *Igreja; carisma e poder.* Rio de Janeiro; Record, 2005.

Cry of the Earth, Cry of the Poor. Maryknoll, NY: Orbis Books, 1995. *Ecologia: grito da Terra; grito dos pobres.* São Paolo: Ática, 2005.

Espiritualidade: um caminho de transformação [Spirituality: A path of transformation]. Rio de Janeiro: Sextante, 2001.

Saint Joseph: The Father of Jesus in a Fatherless Society. Eugene, OR: Cascade Books, 2009. *São Jose: a personificação do Pai.* Campinas: Verus, 2005.

Opção Terra [Option earth]. Rio de Janeiro: Record, 2009.

Proteger a Terra, cuidar da vida [Protect the earth, care for life]. Rio de Janeiro: Record, 2010.

O cuidado necessário [The care needed]. Petropolis: Vozes, 2012.

Also by Leonardo Boff

Cry of the Earth, Cry of the Poor
Ecclesiogenesis: The Base Communities Reinvent the Church
Ecology and Liberation
Faith on the Edge
Francis of Assisi: A Model of Human Liberation
Holy Trinity, Perfect Community
Introducing Liberation Theology (with Clodovis Boff)
Jesus Christ Liberator
Liberating Grace
The Lord Is My Shepherd
The Lord's Prayer
New Evangelization
Passion of Christ, Passion of the World
The Path to Hope
The Prayer of Saint Francis
Praying with Jesus and Mary
Salvation and Liberation (with Clodovis Boff)
The Tao of Liberation (with Mark Hathaway)
Trinity and Society
Way of the Cross, Way of Justice